Pagan
Traditions
of the Holidays

PAGAN TRADITIONS OF THE HOLIDAYS
© 2000 by David Ingraham

Printed in the United States of America

Published by
Bible Belt Publishing
500 Beacon Dr. ▪ Oklahoma City, OK 73127
405/789-1222 ▪ 800/652-1144 ▪ FAX 405/787-2589

ISBN 1-933641-13-3

Pagan Traditions of the Holidays

David Ingraham

Table of Contents

Introduction

Many of our holiday celebrations have their origins in rituals and activities that lie well beyond the boundaries of biblical Christianity. Jesus said of some of His enemies that they strained at a gnat and swallowed a camel, meaning that they often focused on minor issues while ignoring major ones. In preparing the material in this book, we have examined ourselves carefully to be certain that we have not been equally guilty in focusing on occasions in which much family activity takes place, where people have genuine fun and enjoyment, and where, at least in certain circles, the birth of our Savior finds celebration and attention. Still, we are concerned that many Christians have subscribed to celebrating holidays that are *not* Christian, and to celebrating Christian holidays in inappropriate ways.

We have searched our conscience to be confident that the issue before us is of major importance to the body of Christ. Our conclusion: This is no gnat! The Lord has continually confronted paganism throughout Scripture and has stood in direct opposition to it since it originated at the tower of Babel more than four thousand years ago.

In the pages that follow, we will show that much of our Halloween, Christmas, and Easter celebrations originate in paganism. Logic insists that we offend God and compromise our walk with Him by participating in the profane aspects of these holidays. For example, what's wrong with this picture?

It's Easter time at the American Martyrs Roman Catholic Church in Manhattan Beach, Calif., and the Sunday school is hopping. About 350 preschoolers, many sporting freshly crayoned bunny ears, are bouncing about the school hall while their parents attend mass. The "Easter Lady"—a.k.a. Maggie Wright—arrives, dressed in a colorful spring bonnet. "Merry Christmas!" she bellows, to roars of laughter. "I'm here to tell you about Easter, because Easter's kind of confusing." The room quiets down as she begins to tell a story about an ugly little bulb that blossoms into a beautiful flower. Soon the children are up on their feet, reenacting the bulb's transformation into shoot, stem and, finally, flower. "Easter is about how things change," Wright tells them. "What starts to happen in spring? The whole world has died and it is brought back to life. God brings it all back every year!" Satisfied, the preschoolers dash off for the egg hunt. It may not be the Easter story most grown-ups remember learning. But then, most grown-ups didn't go to Sunday school when they were three. Like so many things in our culture—from violin lessons to computer software—religious school is now being tailored to fit even the youngest children. And as in any good nursery school, the learning takes place largely through stories, songs and crafts. "It's little doses of God mixed in with big helpings of fun," says Nancy Pratt, a parent who volunteers at American Martyrs.

—An excerpt from *Play and Pray Newsweek Magazine*, May 15, 2000. "Early religious education can be 'little doses of God mixed in with big helpings of fun," by Susan H. Greenberg and Donna Foote

Our objections to the above are many; however, we find this reference to the "Easter Lady" most objectionable of all. The original Easter Lady has a name—Ishtar. She is the lady who rides the scarlet-colored beast in Revelation 17. Her connection is not to Christ, but to His satanic counterpart—Antichrist. Her connection is to such things as fertility, Mother Earth, and to the worship of nature. The Sunday school activity described above reflects the religious system she exemplifies. Her brand of pantheism is the vehicle by which the New World Order is working to subject the world to a global governance, religion, and economy. She has nothing to do with the resurrection of Christ, and Christians have no business embracing any of her agenda. Yet, we often acquiesce to the religious system she represents. What we once did in ignorance, we can only do by deliberate choice after reading the contents of this book.

Noted Christian author and commentator Berit Kjos offers us this insight:

Throughout history, spiritual compromise has been a constant temptation, and our Easter traditions show the timeless trend toward unholy alliances. While the constant pressure of persecution kept the early Church pure in faith, the shift to cultural acceptance in the Roman empire brought compromise. Then as now, the Christian's goal changed from pleasing God to pleasing man. Soon, the politically correct church had traded purity for popularity and adopted the "abominable" practices of its pagan neighbors. Take a look at some of them:

Easter, the name: According to the *Encyclopaedia Britannica*, "the 8th century derived it from that of the Anglo-Saxon spring goddess Eostre," (Ishtar) whose name, in turn, might have come from "eastre," meaning spring. Once again, pagans honor her as the "goddess of dawn," one of many fertility goddesses celebrated during their spring equinox.

Easter bunny and eggs: According to *The Woman's Dictionary of Symbols & Sacred Objects,* "The Goddess' totem, the Moon-hare, would lay eggs for good children to eat. . . . Eostre's hare was the shape that Celts imaged on the surface of the full moon, derived from old Indo-European sources." While the historical record is too sparse to provide factual details, the Pagan Home Website offers the following description:

"Eostre, a Germanic Goddess, is associated with both spring and sunrise. Tradition has it that Eostre saved a bird whose wings were frozen from the harsh winter by turning it into a magickal, egg-laying hare. Eostre was a maiden whose aspects of renewal and rebirth brought about the reappearance of bright spring flowers, baby chickens fresh from the shell, baby bunnies from their winter dens, and the reoccurrence of the plow in the field. In some European traditions flowers grew from her footprints.

"Pagans lit new fires at dawn to cure ills, renew life and protect the new crops. In some cultures this sacred day included the ringing of bells, singing of songs, and decorating of hard-boiled eggs. Eggs were a symbol of both the sun god (the golden yolk) and fertility (the white shell symbolizing the White Goddess) and were used both as talismans and eaten in ritual. The eggs of wild birds were gathered and these eggs are recreated today with the dyes used in Easter celebrations. The weaving of Easter baskets harks back to the weaving of birds' nests, a necessity prior to egg laying and the continuation of the life cycle."

Hot Cross buns: Some link them to the goddess Eostre, and suggest that the distinctive crossed lines on top represent "Wotan's cross," not the cross of Christ. Others simply attribute the symbol to the Wiccan "quartered circle": four equal lines pointing from the center to the spirits of the north, east, south, and west—or to the basic elements: earth, water, air (or wind), and fire. In Native American traditions, it forms the basic pattern of the medicine wheel and plays a vital part in major rituals.

Countless pagan sites add mythical details that bring life to the bare bones of history. Their stories may tickle the imagination, but they will never bring the wisdom and understanding needed to follow God in a world that has traded truth for myth. The apostle Paul's letter seems as relevant today as ever:

"For the time will come when they will not endure sound doctrine, but according to their own desires, because they have itching ears, they will heap up for themselves teachers; and they will turn their ears away from the truth, and be turned aside to fables. But you be watchful in all things, endure afflictions . . ." (2 Timothy 4:3–5).

—Excerpted from Berit Kjos, *Earth Day Joins Easter*
—*A Sign of Our Times?*, www.Crossroad.to

If the biblical Joshua could address us today as he addressed Israel as they entered the land of Canaan three and a half millennia ago, I believe he would demand of us what he demanded of Israel in that day.

And if it seem evil unto you to serve the LORD, choose you this day whom ye will serve; whether the gods which your fathers served that were on the other side of the flood, or the gods of the Amorites, in whose land ye dwell: but as for me and my house, we will serve the LORD.

—Joshua 24:15

We have a mandate from the Lord to refuse to be conformed to this world but to be transformed by the renewing of our mind (Rom. 12:2). We are equally aware that friendship with the world is enmity with God (Jam. 4:4). Consequently, we have no qualms about presenting the material in this volume.

We are concerned that when the church fails to go into all the world to have an impact on all humanity, the opposite happens. The world finds its way into all the church and impacts the people of God contrary to His Will, His Way, and His Word. The church is like a man on a bicycle: he maintains balance best while making forward progress. He fails and falls when standing still or going backward.

The church that goes into all the world, taking a stand against evil, being branded "intolerant," and refusing to compromise, is a church that *makes* a difference because *it is* different. The church that refuses to allow the culture to shape it is that church which is most likely to shape and impact the culture. Our complicity with and conformity to the paganism of our holiday seasons are examples of the church conforming to the world. Perilous times have come upon our day and age because the Devil has been working diligently while the church slept (Matt. 13:25).

> And that, knowing the time, that now it is high time to awake out of sleep: for now is our salvation nearer than when we believed.
>
> —Romans 13:11

We dedicate this book to that awakening.

Chapter One

Paganism and the Tower of Babel

The Old Testament, among numerous other significant things, is a record of a conflict between the Lord and paganism. We often generalize and say that the battle is that of good versus evil; God versus the Devil; light versus darkness, and so forth. Although all of this is true, specific names, dates, and places attach to these generalizations in the Law, the Writings, and the Prophets, that cause us to focus on particular religious practices. These practices produced spiritual adultery among the ancient people of God and the heathen round about them.

The starting place for all forms of idolatry, nature worship, and occult practices is the tower of Babel. Here, the infamous Nimrod became the leader of a grand rebellion against the revelation of God to his ancestors. Here the notable declension of Romans chapter one took root until the greatness of man's sin required that the nations be divided from each other into races, tribes, and languages.

> And the LORD said, Behold, the people is one, and they have all one language; and this they begin to do: and now nothing will be restrained from them, which they have imagined to do. . . . Therefore is the name of it called Babel; because the LORD did there confound the language of all

the earth: and from thence did the LORD scatter them abroad
upon the face of all the earth.

—Genesis 11:6, 9

Isolated, man's imagination is formidable; corporately, man's imagination is boundless. Our world today offers a portrait of what happens when the effect of the tower of Babel incident becomes removed from man's history. Given the universal use of the English language, and the instant and constant communications now available, a unity of formidable proportions continues to develop. It is bringing the world and knowledge together faster than ever before. With this reversal of the tower of Babel, "nothing will be restrained from them which they [sinful men] have imagined to do."

From Babel, elements of paganism spread across the entire ancient world. Certain elements became predominant to one culture and other elements became common to another culture. The culture of Mesopotamia incorporated the entire package and became the fountainhead from which Babylonianism spread first to Egypt, and, eventually, westward to the Mediterranean and then to Rome.

Mesopotamia included the city of Ur of the Chaldees, the home of Terah and his family. Of his three distinguished sons, Abram (later called Abraham) was the most notable in terms of biblical history. He became the progenitor of the Israeli people and the model of the biblical principle of justification. The story of Abraham is foundational to the grand themes of Scripture.

Here, however, it is his name that bears great weight as we consider his early connection to paganism. The preformative *Ab* in the Hebrew language means "father." Then the balance of the word, *ruom* (*Ab-ruom*) means "lofty or high one."

Thus, the name could mean "father of the high place" or

"my father is a high or lofty one." In either case, both the name and the environment from which they came indicate that Abram was associated, perhaps through his father, with ziggurat worship in the land of ancient Chaldaea. If so, then Abraham and his family may have worshipped either the moon god, Nannar, or the moon goddess, Ishtar.

God called Abram out of this environment. He was to separate himself from his house, his kindred, and the land in which he dwelled. Throughout Scripture, the solution for involvement in paganism is separation. Even in those situations where physical separation is neither practical nor required by the Lord, a separation from the practices and the philosophies of paganism is implicit in the text.

So it is today that Christians may not be able to remove themselves from a heathen environment or to remove pagan practices from their periphery. Nevertheless, holiness demands a separation from the principles and practices embraced by unregenerate people and the religious systems they often represent. We encounter much of these pagan trappings during the holiday seasons. While we may embrace those practices that have a biblical basis, such as the nativity and the resurrection, we dabble with the other symbols and activities common to the holidays at the expense of a distinctively different Christian life.

Abraham eventually found himself a man rich with cattle and goods and the father of two sons, Ishmael and Isaac. When the day came that Isaac required a wife, Abraham contracted with his elder servant, Eliezar, to embark upon a journey into pagan lands to bring a woman back for Isaac. She must not be a woman of the Canaanites, but, instead, a member of Abraham's kindred.

> And the servant said unto him, Peradventure the woman
> will not be willing to follow me unto this land: must I needs

bring thy son again unto the land from whence thou cam-
est? And Abraham said unto him, Beware thou that thou
bring not my son thither again. The Lord God of heaven,
which took me from my father's house, and from the land
of my kindred, and which spake unto me, and that sware
unto me, saying, Unto thy seed will I give this land; he shall
send his angel before thee, and thou shalt take a wife unto
my son from thence. And if the woman will not be willing
to follow thee, then thou shalt be clear from this my oath:
only bring not my son thither again.

—Genesis 24:5–8

The servant returned with Rebekah, sister of Laban, and together she and Isaac generated twin sons, Esau and Jacob.
This next generation also made a return trip to the pagan city
of Haran, where Jacob ultimately found two wives, Leah and
Rachel, daughters of Rebekah's brother, Laban. Uncle Laban
was an idolator—he probably had been when, a generation
before, Eliezer sought a wife for Isaac. Evidently, cousins Leah
and Rachel were idolators also because Rachel conspired to
bring some of Laban's household gods with them into the
Land of Promise.

Jacob's Journey from Haran Back to Canaan

"And Laban went to shear his sheep: and Rachel had stolen
the images that were her father's" (Gen. 31:19). These
gods (Heb. *teraphim*) may have been made of either wood
or clay. Archaeological evidence shows them as simple and
primitive figurines. They may have been associated with the
title deeds to Laban's property because Rachel and Leah
seemed concerned that they had no inheritance in their father's house.

And Rachel and Leah answered and said unto him, Is there
yet any portion or inheritance for us in our father's house?

> Are we not counted of him strangers? for he hath sold us,
> and hath quite devoured also our money.
>
> —Genesis 31:14–15

Believed to be the custodians of human happiness, the teraphim were often worshipped as gods and consulted as mediums (Ezek. 21:21; Zech. 10:2). From the very origins of what later became the people of Israel, idolatry, one of the basic elements of paganism, became a problem to and the ultimate nemesis of the ancient people of God.

For all of his history as a "schemer," Jacob soon appears to be a spiritual giant among his people. Having wrestled with the Angel of the Lord who then names him "Israel," Jacob finds himself cleansing his family and house of the idols that surreptitiously had accompanied him to Canaan.

> And God said unto Jacob, Arise, go up to Bethel, and dwell
> there: and make there an altar unto God, that appeared
> unto thee when thou fleddest from the face of Esau thy
> brother. Then Jacob said unto his household, and to all that
> were with him, Put away the strange gods that are among
> you, and be clean, and change your garments: And let us
> arise, and go up to Bethel; and I will make there an altar
> unto God, who answered me in the day of my distress, and
> was with me in the way which I went. And they gave unto
> Jacob all the strange gods which were in their hand, and
> all their earrings which were in their ears; and Jacob hid
> them under the oak which was by Shechem.
>
> —Genesis 35:1–4

Jacob's life was one of deception and conflict. Nevertheless, when chronological maturity began to combine with spiritual maturity, Jacob became a giant among the people of faith.

His eleventh son, Joseph, entered Egypt as a slave, sold thereunto by his jealous brothers. Years later, Jacob and his remaining sons were forced by famine to join Joseph in what was then a hotbed of pagan culture and worship. Four hundred years later when Moses led the descendents of Jacob and his family out of Egypt, through the wilderness, and into the Promised Land, he led a nation whose background included the domination of paganism.

Redemption Out of a Pagan Culture

If Genesis is the history of the beginning of God's confrontation with the Babylonian religion, then Exodus is the story of a nation's redemption from a culture steeped in all its trappings. With both the blood of the paschal lamb and the power of His redemptive presence, the Lord called His Son, Israel (Hos. 11:1), out of Egypt to become a separated nation, much as He had called Abraham nearly six hundred years earlier.

Paganism is a sensuous indulgence of the flesh. This factor is one of several that makes the allurement of the religion so compelling and so difficult to break. Even when one is able temporarily to break free from its bondage, a continuation in its presence and in its surroundings keeps calling the slave back to its practices and principles.

Faith in the God of Abraham, Isaac, and Jacob has no sensual attractions that bind the flesh in an obsessive and compulsive relationship. To walk by faith and not by sight means that believers in the Lord have no appeals to the senses upon which to acquire and to build their religious edifice. The apostle Paul puts it this way: "While we look not at the things which are seen, but at the things which are not seen: for the things which are seen are temporal; but the things which are not seen are eternal" (2 Cor. 4:18).

Absent from our faith are the sights of pagan idols and such attractive accouterments as flashy jewelry, brightly colored costume, and other spectacular displays such as fire, fireworks, and lights. Few are the sounds of festivity and celebration; the beat of drums, the mantras, the bells and cymbals, the sounds of dance and frivolity prescribed by Scripture. The scent of evergreen boughs, incense, the scent of wine and special festive cuisine are not intrinsic to the faith to which we subscribe. The sexual gratification of fertility rites and goddess worship have no place in Christian life and worship. The mystery, rush, and awe of celestial considerations such as astrology, sun and moon worship, and the like, may make belief in the Savior seem rather bland by comparison. They appeal to the base nature of man and to his five senses. Each sense has the potential of locking the pagan practitioner into bondage from which the only escape is physical, geographical separation. The Lord will not tolerate compromise in the matter and the believer must not have complicity in both systems at the same time:

> And what concord hath Christ with Belial? or what part hath he that believeth with an infidel? And what agreement hath the temple of God with idols? for ye are the temple of the living God; as God hath said, I will dwell in them, and walk in them; and I will be their God, and they shall be my people. Wherefore come out from among them, and be ye separate, saith the Lord, and touch not the unclean thing; and I will receive you, And will be a Father unto you, and ye shall be my sons and daughters, saith the Lord Almighty.
>
> —2 Corinthians 6:15–18

As the children of Israel embarked on their forty-year journey from Egypt to the Promised Land, they met the Lord at Mount Sinai. Here they received what amounted to a tenant–landlord agreement regarding the land of their future habitation. The Mosaic covenant stated the conditional nature of their occupation of the land and required the Israelites to be free of the paganism they had endured more than four hundred years.

The Ten Commandments

"And God spake all these words, saying . . ." (Exod. 20:1). The Decalogue (Ten Commandments) is not merely a collection of prohibitions and mandates. It also constitutes a theological expression of the nature of God Himself. Note what each of the commandments declares about the character of God.

> I am the LORD thy God, which have brought thee out of the land of Egypt, out of the house of bondage. Thou shalt have no other gods before me. Thou shalt not make unto thee any graven image, or any likeness of any thing that is in heaven above, or that is in the earth beneath, or that is in the water under the earth.
>
> —Exodus 20:2–4

While paintings and sculpture may be acceptable among believers, this passage forbids using art as a point of contact for worship. All Scripture is consistent in the condemnation of the worship of any created thing in place of the Creator. The first commandment (vs. 3) forbids worship of other gods; the second commandment (vss. 4–5) forbids the use of visual portrayals of God in worship, or the use of aspects of God's creation as symbols of God in worship.

> Thou shalt not bow down thyself to them, nor serve them: for I the LORD thy God am a jealous God, visiting the iniquity of the fathers upon the children unto the third and fourth generation of them that hate me; And showing mercy unto thousands of them that love me, and keep my commandments. Thou shalt not take the name of the LORD thy God in vain; for the LORD will not hold him guiltless that taketh his name in vain.
>
> —Exodus 20:5–7

The first three of the Ten Commandments all pertain to the idolatry to which Israel had been exposed and the paganism they would confront as they entered the land flowing with milk and honey. These mandates and prohibitions demand that Israel keep its distance from the religions that at that moment dominated Canaan. They will bear striking similarity to those of Egypt with a change of names and some of the details.

The separation required to replace Babylonianism with the worship of God required extermination—genocide of the inhabitants of the land. So, rather than to simply remove His ancient people from an environment of paganism, the Lord will demand that the armies of the redeemed liquidate the residents of the land and thus rid the land of the evil practices prevalent there as Joshua arrived.

> Thou shalt not bow down to their gods, nor serve them, nor do after their works: but thou shalt utterly overthrow them, and quite break down their images.
>
> —Exodus 23:24

The Lord was perfectly clear that the pagan inhabitants of the land were not to co-inhabit the land of Israel:

> And I will set thy bounds from the Red sea even unto the sea of the Philistines, and from the desert unto the river: for I will deliver the inhabitants of the land into your hand; and thou shalt drive them out before thee. Thou shalt make no covenant with them, nor with their gods. They shall not dwell in thy land, lest they make thee sin against me: for if thou serve their gods, it will surely be a snare unto thee.
>
> —Exodus 23:31–33

What makes these commands so impressive is the utter seriousness with which the Lord treated the blight of false religion. Thousands of people died, others seized their property, and the unqualified judgment of God fell upon those who dabbled with this phony, mythological, and legendary system. Yet, modern Christians have no conscience about wearing jewelry celebrating somebody else's religion, adorning their homes with figurines, amulets, and other decorative items, or celebrating pagan holidays with symbols and accouterments suitable for worshipping false deities and celebrating pagan festivals. Such items include Easter eggs, hot crossed buns, Halloween archetypes such as black cats, bats, jack o'lanterns, and evergreen trees and wreaths. None of these items has any connection to Christ or to Christianity, yet we display them annually with scarcely a thought about what they in reality represent. It's not a sin to display a black cat; the sin lies in our failure to separate from pagan principles and practices.

Within twelve chapters of the giving of the Law and a commitment from the people saying, "All that the Lord hath spoken we will do," a most revealing incident took place within the wilderness camp.

The Golden Calf

And when the people saw that Moses delayed to come down out of the mount, the people gathered themselves together unto Aaron, and said unto him, Up, make us gods, which shall go before us; for as for this Moses, the man that brought us up out of the land of Egypt, we wot not what is become of him. And Aaron said unto them, Break off the golden earrings, which are in the ears of your wives, of your sons, and of your daughters, and bring them unto me. And all the people brake off the golden earrings which were in their ears, and brought them unto Aaron. And he received them at their hand, and fashioned it with a graving tool, after he had made it a molten calf: and they said, These be thy gods, O Israel, which brought thee up out of the land of Egypt. And when Aaron saw it, he built an altar before it; and Aaron made proclamation, and said, To morrow is a feast to the LORD. And they rose up early on the morrow, and offered burnt offerings, and brought peace offerings; and the people sat down to eat and to drink, and rose up to play.

—Exodus 32:1–6

A sacred bull or calf was common to pagan fertility religion. In disobedience of Yahweh's command in chapter twenty, verses four through six, the people seem to have equated Him with this calf (vs. 5). The allurement of paganism must have been overwhelming to this fledgling nation and its spiritually immature individuals. They returned to the familiar, the sensual, and the comfortable. Moreover, the Hebrew verb translated "play" may refer, as here, to sexual activities (Gen. 26:8), which frequently dominated the fertility cults of the pagan nations.

Throughout the Pentateuch, the Lord reiterates His commandment concerning any flirtation with the idols and practices of the heathen. He even prohibits intermarriage or any compromise whatever with the Gentiles who will be dispossessed of their lands, their property, and of life itself.

When the LORD thy God shall bring thee into the land whither thou goest to possess it, and hath cast out many nations before thee, the Hittites, and the Girgashites, and the Amorites, and the Canaanites, and the Perizzites, and the Hivites, and the Jebusites, seven nations greater and mightier than thou; And when the LORD thy God shall deliver them before thee; thou shalt smite them, and utterly destroy them; thou shalt make no covenant with them, nor show mercy unto them: Neither shalt thou make marriages with them;

thy daughter thou shalt not give unto his son, nor his daughter shalt thou take unto thy son.

> —Deuteronomy 7:1–3 (cf. Gen. 24:3;
> 1 Kings 11:1ff.; 2 Cor. 6:14–18)

The issue that the Lord confronts is the preservation of the tiny nation, Israel. Through this seemingly unlikely people, the Lord will inaugurate a Kingdom that will never be destroyed. This dubious assembly will become the custodians of the revelation of God to all humanity by means of the Holy Scriptures. Then, in His ultimate act of redemption for fallen man, it will be through Israel that the Seed of the Woman promised in Genesis 3:15 and amplified in Genesis 49:10, will come to seek and to save that which was lost.

Offstage, a sinister enemy of God will have a tremendous and eternal stake in derailing the redemptive plan of God. Behind the scenes, a battle of infinite dimensions for the souls of men and women is fully in progress as the Lord issues His law regarding any concessions to or complicity with the religion of Nimrod and his progeny. So, with only this brief but pungent word of explanation, the Lord through Moses explains the necessity for extermination of the enemy and for total victory over them: "For they will turn away thy son from following me, that they may serve other gods: so will the anger of the Lord be kindled against you, and destroy thee suddenly" (Deut 7:4).

Upon entering the land, Israel must fill a prescription from their God to eliminate both present and future danger to His people:

> But thus shall ye deal with them; ye shall destroy their altars, and break down their images, and cut down their groves, and burn their graven images with fire. For thou art an holy people unto the Lord thy God: the Lord thy God

hath chosen thee to be a special people unto himself, above all people that are upon the face of the earth.

—Deuteronomy 7:5–6

Holiness was to be characteristic of Israel; likewise, it is to be characteristic of the church (cf. 1 Thess. 4:3–8).

In addition to the idolatry, nature worship, fertility rites, and the worship of celestial bodies, the Babylonians developed occult practices which the Lord termed "abominations." We will enlarge upon these items elsewhere, but as important as it is to identify the practices is the matter of understanding why they deserved the prohibitions they received: "When thou art come into the land which the LORD thy God giveth thee, thou shalt not learn to do after the abominations of those nations" (Deut. 18:9).

Verses nine through thirteen of Deuteronomy 18 tell the people that they were not to try to discern God's will as the pagans did. Rather in verses fourteen through twenty-two we find they would be given prophets of the Lord. The sacrificing of children (such as to Molech, cf. Lev. 20:2–5; Acts 7:43) was particularly detestable to the Lord. Perhaps equally detestable to Him is the modern practice of abortion—sacrificing children on the altar of convenience, materialism, and self-indulgence. The other practices mentioned involved using means such as observing natural phenomena, using drugs or incantations, or calling upon the dead to determine or control the future.

There shall not be found among you any one that maketh his son or his daughter to pass through the fire, or that useth divination, or an observer of times, or an enchanter, or a witch, Or a charmer, or a consulter with familiar spirits, or a wizard, or a necromancer. For all that do these things are an abomination unto the LORD: and because of these abominations the LORD thy God doth drive them out from before thee.

—Deuteronomy 18:10–12

Most of these practices involved an attempt to discern the will of God or His plan for the future. While many of these erroneous practices continue into modern times, they illustrate for us that there is a right way and a wrong way to determine the will and the way of God.

> Thou shalt be perfect with the LORD thy God. For these nations, which thou shalt possess, hearkened unto observers of times, and unto diviners: but as for thee, the LORD thy God hath not suffered thee so to do.
>
> —Deuteronomy 18:13–14

Note well that both the practices and those who practice them now merit the description "abomination" so far as the Lord is concerned. In addition, the Lord prohibits Israel from following their example. The Lord does not redeem His people from idolatry here only to abandon them to idolatry there. Nor does He purge a land of evil today in order to deliver it into the hands of evil tomorrow. Nor does the Lord redeem us simply *in* our sin; He redeems us *from* our sin as well. If His treatment of pagans seems harsh, crude, or unloving, remember that the issues are eternal in significance and infinite in scope. The battle is visible in one dimension; but only the invisible battle in another dimension can explain the violence and severity of the Lord's actions toward this egregious religious system. The Devil and his formidable forces have incorporated fallen man into the fray to their unfortunate destruction. Remember, they had a choice in the matter and they chose the wrong way.

So, now that we have determined the wrong way to determine the things of God, we now turn to the way prescribed of God in the next several verses: "The LORD thy God will raise up unto thee a Prophet from the midst of thee, of thy brethren, like unto me; unto him ye shall hearken" (Deut. 18:15).

A line of prophets beginning with Samuel three hundred years later would establish contact between Israel and the Lord. However, the ultimate fulfillment of the prophecy is Messiah—the Lord Jesus. Israel was under orders from the Lord to heed these prophets who would rise up from the ranks of Israel with the anointing of God upon them.

Among the characteristics of a true prophet is the flawless accuracy of his predictions of the future.

> When a prophet speaketh in the name of the LORD, if the thing follow not, nor come to pass, that is the thing which the LORD hath not spoken, but the prophet hath spoken it presumptuously: thou shalt not be afraid of him.
>
> —Deuteronomy 18:22

In addition, they boldly warned the people of Divine judgment while reminding them of God's love and the promises He guaranteed. Unlike a priest or king, the prophet did not inherit his office nor gain it by human appointment. In fact, he held no official office at all because the word "prophet" describes his function rather than his position. The Lord had no limitations on whom He might call to speak for Him; a peasant, priest, king, or even a woman could be eligible, depending upon the Lord who calls and empowers.

> According to all that thou desiredst of the LORD thy God in Horeb in the day of the assembly, saying, Let me not hear again the voice of the LORD my God, neither let me see this great fire any more, that I die not. And the LORD said unto me, They have well spoken that which they have spoken. I

will raise them up a Prophet from among their brethren, like unto thee, and will put my words in his mouth; and he shall speak unto them all that I shall command him. And it shall come to pass, that whosoever will not hearken unto my words which he shall speak in my name, I will require it of him.

—Deuteronomy 18:16–19

Obedience to the prophet was obligatory; failure to comply resulted in corporate or individual culpability or both according to the above.

The prophet also was accountable to God for delivering the message and doing so faithfully. His life depended on his accuracy; his accuracy depended on the Lord. Consequently, Israel enjoyed a consistent vision from the Lord for hundreds of years. God validated His prophet by validating His prophecy. Many of these spokesmen for the Lord contributed to the canon of Scripture where, over a period of some fifteen hundred years, they revealed the plans, purposes, and programs of God.

The quality of their message, the loftiness of their rhetoric, the consistency of the themes that dominated their writings, and the unmistakable imprint of Divine inspiration, distanced them from the primitive prognostications that may have risen from the Babylonian mystics. In fact, nothing in all of ancient literature can match the integrity and the simplicity of Scripture. The multiplicity of texts, dated in antiquity, attest to the distribution of the Bible and to the reverence in which it was held since the earliest of times.

The passages prohibiting occult dabblings with paranormal experiences, instead of being restrictive and limiting, were gracious regulations that limited the fraudulent and elevated the legitimate. As usual, the forbidden fruit is most appealing, but its reward is most appalling.

"Choose you this day . . ."

Joshua received instruction from the Lord to exterminate the Canaanites in the Land of Promise. Although his intentions were honorable and his desire was to serve the Lord, he failed to achieve this objective. The consequences of that failure became one of the major themes of Israelite history—the continual contest between Baal and the Lord for the souls of the sons and daughters of Jacob.

Among his failures was the deception perpetrated upon Joshua and company by the Gibeonites, idolators who saved their own lives by selling themselves into virtual slavery to the invading armies of Israel. But their presence among the people of God coupled with that of other inhabitants of Canaan who survived the invasion, became a thorn in the side for the spiritual life of the new nation, Israel. Eventually, the Canaanite religion, a product of Babylonianism, competed with and often superseded the worship of the Lord in the land He promised to Abraham, Isaac, and Jacob.

The day finally came when the occupation of the land was complete, and the parcels of land allotted to each individual tribe had been so distributed. It was here that Joshua gave the people this notable choice:

> And if it seem evil unto you to serve the LORD, choose you this day whom ye will serve; whether the gods which your fathers served that were on the other side of the flood, or the gods of the Amorites, in whose land ye dwell: but as for me and my house, we will serve the LORD.
>
> —Joshua 24:15

Note well that Joshua was demanding that they worship the Lord; if not, then they had to choose which pagan gods they would serve. Someone has said:

> Our contemporary pluralistic society presents us with a con-

fusing display of values, goals, and lifestyles. It is not a god-less society, but a society full of gods pleading for our attention. The issue is whether to obey our mighty and loving Creator, or to be lost in a hell-bound madhouse of confusion.

One can almost envision the aged warrior marking out a line in the sand with the toe of his sandal and demanding of his people that they take their stand and make their decision. His stand was clear, "As for me and my house, we will serve the Lord."

Chapter Two

Rain On Your Easter Parade

The preacher greeted his Easter morning crowd with a cheerful, "Merry Christmas!" When the twittering and chuckling finally settled, he explained that since he would not see many of today's flock again until next Easter, he wanted to give them a holiday greeting in advance.

Although its commercial value pales in comparison to Christmas, Easter is the most important holiday on the church calender. Attendance is traditionally higher on Easter Sunday than on any other day. Sermons and lessons on the resurrection of Christ abound from the pulpit to ears that may not hear it again until next year.

Easter bonnets, Easter bunnies, Easter lilies, Easter eggs, baby chickens, and hot cross buns all lend their ornamentation to the day when Christendom celebrates the resurrection of Christ. Nothing is so central to church doctrine as the event thus celebrated: "And if Christ be not risen, then is our preaching vain, and your faith is also vain. . . . And if Christ be not raised, your faith is vain; ye are yet in your sins" (1 Cor. 15:14, 17).

So what is the connection between the foregoing ornaments of Easter such as rabbits, buns, and eggs, and the resurrection of our Lord? The answer to that question may rain upon your Easter parade.

Easter in Babylon

The first hint of something amiss is the word "Easter." Almost any resource material will cite a Teutonic goddess by a similar name, "Eostre" or "Eastre."

> Eostre was the deity of both the dawn and spring, and "the pagan symbol of fertility." At her festival in April, sacred fires were lighted on the hills, especially in the Nordic lands. (At this same season, ancient Romans observed the Feast of the Vernal Equinox.)
> —Mamie R. Krythe, *All About American Holidays*, p. 98

Further investigation of this Teutonic name traces it back to Ostera, then Astarte, then to Ishtar (once pronounced as we do "Easter"). Since Ishtar, whose alternate name is Semiramis, was the wife of Nimrod, the priest and king of Babylon, we can trace a direct line between the word "Easter" and the origins of pagan religion.

According to legend, when Nimrod died he proceeded to become the sun-god, while Semiramis (Easter) proceeded to have an illegitimate son, Tammuz, whom she claimed was the son of her deified Nimrod. She apparently claimed Tammuz was the promised seed of the woman (Gen. 3:15) and demanded worship for both herself as well as Tammuz. With only slight effort one can imagine that the mother soon was worshiped as much or more than her bastard son. Tammuz was later symbolized by a golden calf as the son of the sun-god, Nimrod (Ralph Woodrow, *Babylon: Mystery Religion*, pp. 9–10; Exod. 32:1–6). Moreover, when we discover where and how the blessed Mother originated, the plot both thickens and worsens!

As the legend continues, an egg of wondrous size fell from heaven one day and landed in the Euphrates River. Some equally wondrous fishes managed to roll the egg to shore, whereupon several doves descended from heaven and incubated the remarkable find. Soon, out popped Ishtar (or Semiramis), the goddess of Easter. The egg eventually became the universal symbol for fertility, and as such can be traced in pagan cultures worldwide (Woodrow, p. 153). Predictably, it also became the symbol of the goddess herself.

Therefore, at the very least we have traced both the name "Easter" and an element of its celebration, the "Ishtar Egg," to Babylon. Most significantly, both the egg and its hatchling predate the resurrection of Christ by more than two thousand years, eliminating any possible connection among eggs, Easter, and Jesus.

During that two thousand years, Babylonian paganism spread worldwide. It was of this heathen religious system that the apostle Paul wrote in Romans 1:21–23:

> Because that, when they knew God, they glorified him not as God, neither were thankful; but became vain in their imaginations, and their foolish heart was darkened. Professing themselves to be wise, they became fools, And changed the glory of the uncorruptible God into an image made like to corruptible man, and to birds, and four-footed beasts, and creeping things.

This religion became the diabolical substitute for biblical truth. Satan cleverly counterfeited truth with an insidious lie, perverting the minds and cultures of men who suppressed the truth in unrighteousness. Then, just as truth personified in Jesus became both knowable and known, the deceiver wedded Babylonian paganism to the church. The church syncretized the celebration of Easter with the resurrection of Christ.

Babylonian folklore claimed that Tammuz was worshiped during the spring. However, after he was slain, his mother (Easter) so wept that he came alive again. The manifestation of his "resurrected" life was the arrival of vegetation in the spring. When Jesus arose in the spring following His crucifixion, logic seemed to dictate a connection between the ignominious fable and the glorious fact. Then, when the church later desired to become popular with both pagan and saint, it amalgamated the celebration of Jesus' resurrection with the fertility rites, eggs, and other accouterments of a pagan holiday.

After all, Easter celebrated the arrival of spring, the resurrection of life from the dead of winter. What could be more appropriate?

Easter in the Early Church

Early Christians celebrated Resurrection Day on the same day as the Jewish Passover, regardless of the day of the week on which it fell. However, when Gentiles became prominent in the early church, they required the celebration to fall on Sunday. A major conflict ensued contributing to the rift between the eastern and western branches of the church.

The Emperor Constantine called the Council of Nicaea in 325 A.D. The question of the date of Easter was one of its main concerns. The council decided that Easter should fall on Sunday following the first full moon after the vernal equinox. The astronomically astute Alexandrians were given the job of computing the date. Additional difficulties were overcome when March 21 was chosen as the date of the vernal equinox. . . . The dating of Easter today follows the

Nicene reckoning. The Eastern Orthodox Church stipulates
in addition that Easter must fall after Passover.
                              —Robert Myers, *Celebrations: The Complete
                              Book of American Holidays*, pp. 102–103)

Because the Eastern Orthodox Church continues to use the
Julian calendar for religious holidays, rather than the Grego-
rian calendar used in our western culture, it celebrates Easter thirteen days later than Roman churches and other western churches. The Roman church developed a high Mass for
celebrating the resurrection of Christ, but attached to it much
of the paganism of the spring festival. Included in this package was the forty-day season of fasting known as "Lent,"
adopted by Rome during the sixth century. It corresponds to
a forty-day fast practiced by ancient Egyptians. Others identify Lent with a practice among Babylonian worshipers of
Semiramis. The death and resurrection of Tammuz was celebrated by a great annual festival preceded by a Lenten fast
(Russell Tardo, *Rabbits, Eggs, and Other Easter Errors*, pp.
13–14).

For the next thousand years of western history, little
changed within Catholicism. Only with the Reformation came
changes in Easter celebrations as Protestantism grew in size
and influence.

Easter in America

By the time Puritans came from England to America they
had dropped the celebration of holy days such as Christmas
and Easter. Their influence limited all such celebrations in
the colonies. Only after the Civil War did Easter services become prominent again in America.

Perhaps it was the deep scars of death and destruction
which led people back to the Easter season. The story of

the Resurrection was a logical inspiration of renewed hope
for all those bereaved by the war.
                                —Robert Myers, *Celebrations,* p. 104

Meanwhile, isolated pockets of celebrants continued to recognize Easter in America. In 1741, Moravian believers began a long-standing custom of sunrise services, complete with
trombone, choir, and singers. In California in 1770, Father
Crespi, a Francisan monk, celebrated an Easter sunrise service under the Cathedral Oak, marked today by an historical
plaque. Theodore Roosevelt held a well-known sunrise service on Mount Rubidoux in California in 1909, and the Hollywood Bowl became host to the annual sunrise event in 1921.
In the Wichita Mountains of Oklahoma, the Passion Play, six
hours in length, begins at midnight of Easter morning. One
hundred thousand people annually attend the play (Myers,
Celebrations p. 107).

Easter Ornaments
Originating in paganism, propagated by a faltering church,
then traditionalized by a burgeoning American continent, Easter eventually became firmly entrenched in the culture of the
United States. With it came its pagan embellishments. Most
Americans embrace these ornamentations of the season without questioning their significance. When confronted, some
find the exposure of their error both intrusive and offensive;
others become incensed by their own negligence in adopting
such heathen trappings.

Perhaps the most common ornament of Easter is the
brightly colored, hard-boiled egg. Given its previously cited
Babylonian origins, the Easter egg's rise in significance and
popularity over the millennia is not surprising.

Eggs have become closely associated with Easter, and are
regarded as a symbol of resurrection, for they hold the seeds

of life, and represent the revival of fertility upon the earth. However, the egg as a life emblem is much older than Christianity.

—Krythe, *All About American Holidays*, p. 103

Cultures worldwide have myths describing how the universe originated from an egg. Among some peoples, the "Heavenly One" once inhabited an egg which he broke in two, with one half becoming gold, the other half silver. The gold elements became the sky, the silver elements the earth. The outer membrane became the atmosphere, the veins became rivers, and the fluid became oceans (Myers, *Celebrations*, pp. 110–111).

Egg painting may have originated in Persia and Egypt centuries ago. When the custom migrated into Europe, possibly by way of the Knights of the Crusades, egg decorating became an elaborate art.

Often the eggs were dipped in red dye, but in Hungary there were more white ones with patterns of red flowers. Yugoslav people have usually marked their eggs with X V, standing for "Christ is risen.". . .

Women and girls of Poland and the south of Russia always began working weeks ahead on eggs covered all over with designs. There would be lines that crisscrossed, tiny checkerboards, patterns of dots and plant and animal shapes. No two eggs were alike but the same symbols appeared again and again. A sun was for good luck, a hen or rooster to make wishes come true, a deer for good health, and flowers for love and beauty.

—Edna Barth, *Lilies, Rabbits, and Painted Eggs: The Story of the Easter Symbols*, pp. 28–29)

Eggs have been given as gifts, eaten for fertility purposes, rolled down hills, thrown into the air, used for play, hidden on church lawns and grounds, hung about the neck to ward off evil, and worshiped as a source of life. No legitimate connection exists between any such practices and the resurrection of Christ from the dead.

Everybody knows that rabbits don't lay eggs, but the relationship between these two Easter phenomena is indisputable.

> To be perfectly correct, it is the hare, not the rabbit, who should be honored as the most famous secular Easter symbol. . . . Easter is a movable feast dependent for its date on the phase of the moon, and from antiquity the hare has been a symbol for the moon; the rabbit has not. Hares are born with their eyes open, rabbits are born blind; the Egyptian name for the hare was Un, meaning "open" or "to open," and the full moon watched open-eyed through out the night. According to legend, the hare was thought never to blink or close its eyes.
>
> —Barth, *Lilies, Rabbits, and Painted Eggs*, p. 51

The harlot of Revelation 17 symbolizes the religion of Babylon. She is nothing less than the moon goddess worshiped in ziggurats and towers of the ancient Middle East. Her name likely is Ishtar (Easter). To our disgrace, she has invaded and defiled what are purported to be celebrations of the resurrection of Christ. She does so through her ancient representatives, the Easter bunny and the Easter egg.

Associated with fertility and reproduction is the Easter lily.

> The fragrant, waxy white flower we call the Easter lily is not a spring flower or an American flower at all. A lily growing on islands near Japan was taken to Bermuda and then traveled to the United States to become our most special

Easter plant. Flower growers have learned how to make it bloom in time.

—Barth, *Lilies, Rabbits, and Painted Eggs*, p. 51

Tardo adds:

Having become symbolic of the season, churches world-wide decorate their altars with these beautiful flowers, and innumerable thousands of them are given away to women at Easter as gifts. Few, however, realize the ancient significance of such gifts! The so-called "Easter lily" has long been revered by pagans of various lands as a holy symbol associated with the reproductive organs. It was considered a phallic symbol! One might easily surmise what was being suggested by sending a gift of such nature in ancient times.

—Tardo, *Rabbits, Eggs, and Other Easter Errors*, pp. 11–12

Even the sunrise service originates not in Christianity but in the pagan rites of spring.

Sunrise services are not unrelated to the Easter fires held on the tops of hills in continuation of the New Year fires, a worldwide observance in antiquity. Rites were performed at the vernal equinox welcoming the sun and its great power to bring new life to all growing things.

—Robert Myers, *Celebrations*, p. 105

Although the hot cross bun is often associated with Good Friday, its real significance pertains to Easter. One of the stories remaining in tradition today relates the origin of this bun:

. . . back to the ancient pagan custom of *worshiping the Queen of Heaven with offerings of cakes marked with her image.* It is said that the Egyptians made buns with two horns on them to offer to the *moon goddess,* and that the Greeks changed the symbol to a cross so the bun could be more easily divided. Anglo-Saxons marked theirs with a cross to honor the goddess of light [emphasis mine].

> —Krythe, *All About American Holidays,* pp. 94–95)

The prophet Jeremiah apparently referred to this raisin cake:

> The children gather wood, and the fathers kindle the fire, and the women knead their dough, *to make cakes to the queen of heaven,* and to pour out drink offerings unto other gods, that they may provoke me to anger."
>
> —Jer. 7:18; see also 44:17–19, 25–26)

This Queen of Heaven's name is Ishtar (Easter). Hot cross buns are a veiled ascription of worship to her. By consuming them, we participate in pagan Babylonianism. Little wonder the Bible says to us: ". . . Come out of her, my people, that ye be not partakers of her sins, *and that ye receive not of her plagues"* (Rev. 18:4).

The wearing of Easter finery, new clothing and hats, and the so-called Easter parade originated in heathenism. Easter fires are a leftover from spring rites. Ham for Easter is an English tradition expressing, of all things, bigotry toward Jews.

Without exception, the ornaments of Easter are pagan in origin. Informed Christians who continue in these traditions and practices risk for themselves the consternation of God.

Scripture abounds with numerous references to the idolatry spawned in Babylon. It was worship of the Babylonian goddess that brought Israel to ruin. Later in biblical history, when Christians began to mingle paganism with worship, the apostle Paul addressed the matter in this way:

Be ye not unequally yoked together with unbelievers: for what fellowship hath righteousness with unrighteousness? And what communion hath light with darkness? And what concord hath Christ with Belial? or what part hath he that believeth with an infidel?

—2 Cor. 6:14–15

The most notable passage addressing this religious system is also the passage that connects its practices to the world in which we live today. Romans 1 describes the societal declension that results from removing the true God from His rightful place and prominence. Replacing the truth of God with a lie always conveys predictable consequences. The sexual revolution and the decline of western culture give us the spiritual signs of our times:

Wherefore God also gave them up to uncleanness through the lusts of their own hearts, to dishonor their own bodies between themselves: Who changed the truth of God into a lie, and worshiped and served the creature more than the Creator, who is blessed for ever. Amen.

—Rom. 1:24–25

The creature of veneration today is man; humanism has made an idol of *self*. The most obvious expression of this occupation with self comes next:

For this cause God gave them up unto vile affections: for even their women did change the natural use into that which is against nature: And likewise also the men, leaving the natural use of the woman, burned in their lust one toward another; men with men working that which is unseemly, and receiving in themselves that recompense of their error which was meet.

—Rom. 1:26–27

The downward spiral of paganism reaches into the most vital of our culture carriers: education. And since the world no longer retains God in its education, the results speak for themselves:

> And even as they did not like to retain God in their knowledge, God gave them over to a reprobate mind, to do those things which are not convenient; Being filled with all unrighteousness, fornication, wickedness, covetousness, maliciousness; full of envy, murder, debate, deceit, malignity; whisperers, Backbiters, haters of God, despiteful, proud, boasters, inventors of evil things, disobedient to parents, Without understanding, covenantbreakers, without natural affection, implacable, unmerciful: Who knowing the judgment of God, that they which commit such things are worthy of death, not only do the same, but have pleasure in them that do them.
>
> —Rom. 1:28–32

If you find yourself characterized in some way in the above passages of scripture (and most of us *do*, to some extent), please recognize that all of mankind has been tainted by this reprobate mind. The only institution of God given to overcome the slippery slope of paganism is the church of Jesus Christ. The church, however, finds itself in various levels of complicity with its pagan adversary depending on the extent to which it participates in what are undeniably pagan practices.

Furthermore, as individuals we must respond appropriately to the light given us. Willful sin which follows such enlightenment makes the sinner even more culpable before God.

The Bible teaches that sin and reprobation are universal problems. Considering that the God of Scripture is holy and absolutely righteous, we each stand condemned before Him.

It's a condition only He could solve and only because He wanted to do so.

Nearly two thousand years ago God sent His Son, Jesus of Nazareth, born of a virgin and without sin, to die on a cross. He represented millions of people in His death; He even represented *you!* Because He didn't deserve to die *ever,* His death became the penalty paid for *all* our sin. He was the sacrificial Lamb of God, the innocent One slain on behalf of the guilty.

If you will simply identify with Him, claim the forgiveness He offers, and trust Him as Savior and Lord, you may this very moment receive life. Bow your head and pray something like this: Lord Jesus, I recognize that as a sinner I need a Savior. I believe that when you died on the cross, you died for me personally. Wash away my sins, give me your eternal life, and help me to be clean before God all the days of this life and in the life to come. Amen.

Chapter Three
The Biblical Account of Paganism

The biblical account of paganism is much too extensive for anything but cursory examination here. However, the enormity of the problem and the preoccupation of the biblical narrative with the subject indicate its importance. The first five hundred years of existence for the nation Israel saw paganism mostly in the outer periphery of society.

With the advent of the monarchy, however, the locus of centrality began to shift from the peasantry into the upper echelons of power. We first see King Saul dabbling with necromancy in his encounter with the witch of Endor. Then, in the reigns of David and Solomon, the introduction of multiple wives and concubines from pagan lands and peoples begins to result in the satanic infiltration of the monarchy with those forms of religion from which the land was to have been liberated under the prowess of Joshua and Caleb centuries before.

While David maintained a consistent distance from the religious influences of the heathen, his son, Solomon, did not. The apostasy that eventually resulted in Israel's ruin, division, and deportation began when paganism reached the summit of influence and power: the royal family of David.

Solomon's Heart Turns from the Lord

But king Solomon loved many strange women, together with the daughter of Pharaoh, women of the Moabites, Ammonites, Edomites, Zidonians, and Hittites; Of the nations concerning which the LORD said unto the children of Israel, Ye shall not go in to them, neither shall they come in unto you: for surely they will turn away your heart after their gods: Solomon clave unto these in love. And he had seven hundred wives, princesses, and three hundred concubines: and his wives turned away his heart. For it came to pass, when Solomon was old, that his wives turned away his heart after other gods: and his heart was not perfect with the LORD his God, as was the heart of David his father.

—1 Kings 11:1–4

The Bible does not state that Solomon openly practiced idolatry. Nevertheless, by his polygamous marriages among Gentile women, he brought such practices into the land with great prominence. He certainly allowed his heathen wives to practice their religious activities and provided the implements and accommodations they needed for doing so. Whether by act or by association, Solomon endorsed evil in the highest, most visible household of the land. A king in his palace or a president in his White House is a role model of the most influential sort, whether for good or for evil.

For Solomon went after Ashtoreth the goddess of the Zidonians, and after Milcom the abomination of the Ammonites. And Solomon did evil in the sight of the LORD, and went not fully after the LORD, as did David his father. Then did Solomon build an high place for Chemosh, the abomination of Moab, in the hill that is before Jerusalem, and for Molech, the abomination of the children of Ammon. And likewise did he for all his strange wives, which burnt incense and sacrificed unto their gods. And the LORD was angry with Solomon, because his heart was turned from the LORD God of Israel, which had appeared unto him twice. And had commanded him concerning this thing, that he should not go after other gods: but he kept not that which the LORD commanded. Wherefore the LORD said unto Solomon, Forasmuch as this is done of thee, and thou hast not kept my covenant and my statutes, which I have commanded thee, I will surely rend the kingdom from thee, and will give it to thy servant.

—1 Kings 11:5–11

Solomon was a man of great privilege, not only because he was king, but because the Lord had appeared to him on two occasions. Despite all this, Solomon deliberately disobeyed the commandment of the Lord that he refrain from idolatry.

In addition, both David and Solomon had a deep and long-lasting relationship with Hiram, the king of Tyre. This king was a Phoenician, and his ties to the religion of Babylon were extensive and pervasive.

Dius, the Phoenician historian, and Menander of Ephesus assign to Hiram a prosperous reign of thirty-four years and relate that his father was Abibal and his son and successor Baleazar. Others (later writers, as Eusebius, after Tatian, Proep. Ev. 10.11) relate that Hiram, besides supplying timber for the Temple, gave his daughter in marriage to Solomon.

—Unger's New Talking Bible Dictionary, "Hiram"

Note well the names Abibal and Baleazar, and the "Bal" in the suffix of one name and in the prefix of the other. Such references either to Bal or Bel remind us of the names given to Bel-shazzar, a grandson of Nebuchadnezzar, and Belteshazzar, the Babylonian name given to Daniel. In both cases these names reflect the god of Babylon, Bel, or Bal, or the elongated, but linguistically identical "Baal."

That Hiram was religiously a pagan, tied to the gods of Babylon, and an observer of times, constellations, and similar religious practices, is not in question. What would be interesting to us is the extent of that influence upon Solomon and his successors to the Davidic throne. Even more interesting might be an investigation into the influence Hiram may have had when an Ephraimite named Jeroboam led the northern ten tribes into rebellion against the Davidic dynasty after 931 B.C.

Jeroboam, King of the Northern Tribes

Immediately upon his ascension to the throne, Jeroboam initiated pagan worship, erecting golden calves at both Bethel and at Dan, reminiscent of the golden calf erected in the wilderness under the leadership of Aaron.

> Then Jeroboam built Shechem in mount Ephraim, and dwelt therein; and went out from thence, and built Penuel. And Jeroboam said in his heart, Now shall the kingdom return to the house of David: If this people go up to do sacrifice in the house of the LORD at Jerusalem, then shall the heart of this people turn again unto their lord, even unto Rehoboam king of Judah, and they shall kill me, and go again to Rehoboam king of Judah. Whereupon the king took counsel, and made two calves of gold, and said unto them, It is too much for you to go up to Jerusalem: behold thy gods, O Israel, which brought thee out of the land of Egypt. And he set the one in Bethel, and the other put he in Dan. And this thing became a sin: for the people went to worship before the one, even unto Dan. And he made an house of high places, and made priests of the lowest of the people, which were not of the sons of Levi.
>
> —1 Kings 12:25–31

The "shrines" probably denote local sanctuaries containing the images of the golden calves or their altars. One reason for not using Levites, as required by Mosaic Law, for priests in the religious centers, was that most had gone to Judah, apparently in rebellion against these religious innovations (2 Chron. 11:13–14).

> And Jeroboam ordained a feast in the eighth month, on the fifteenth day of the month, like unto the feast that is in Judah, and he offered upon the altar. So did he in Bethel, sacrificing unto the calves that he had made: and he placed in Bethel the priests of the high places which he had made.
>
> —1 Kings 12:32

Jeroboam made provision for an annual feast that would substitute for the divinely appointed Feast of Tabernacles, and he set the time for its observance to be one month later.

> So he offered upon the altar which he had made in Bethel the fifteenth day of the eighth month, even in the month which he had devised of his own heart; and ordained a feast unto the children of Israel: and he offered upon the altar, and burnt incense.
>
> —1 Kings 12:33

The king became concerned that pilgrimages to Judah and Jerusalem for religious observances would be detrimental to their loyalty to him. He feared that the return to God-ordained worship might attract his northern people back to the south and so weaken their allegiance to the north. By building these sacred calves, Jeroboam hoped to keep his people united and insulated from other influence.

The calves doubtless were fashioned after the Egyptian sacred bull Apis. He placed them in the extreme north at Dan and in the south at Bethel (1 Kings 12:29). The carefully chosen locations precluded travel into the southern kingdom. The willingness of thousands of Israelites to accept this idolatrous perversion of worship indicates the degree to which many of them already were disposed to abandon the worship of the Lord. Evidently, paganism had been influencing them over the nearly six centuries since the Exodus, and a return to a worldly, Egyptian religion may have been but a relatively small step for them to take.

> Ye adulterers and adulteresses, know ye not that the friendship of the world is enmity with God? whosoever therefore will be a friend of the world is the enemy of God.
>
> —James 4:4

Therefore, if our aversion to the accoutrements of today's holiday seasons seems overdone or exaggerated, consider these ten northern tribes. They had been separated from a totally pagan environment for a dozen generations. By comparison, in our century we would go back to the mid-fifteenth century, long before the discovery of America by Columbus to equal the same interval of time. On the one hand, the people had forgotten the days of Moses and the supernatural deliverance from Egypt experienced by their ancestors. The excitement of conquest and the newness of a land flowing with milk and honey had become rather humdrum and matter-of-fact over a half millennia. The zest and zeal of their worship of the Lord had perhaps by this time yielded to a perfunctory, mechanical liturgy. All of this may have contributed to what may have become an indifference to the things of the Lord and His service.

Yet, it was their continued dabbling and trifling with the profane that desensitized them to its evil. By intermarrying with foreigners, wearing amulets and jewelry reminiscent of

paganism, decorating houses and property with images, figurines, and other icons, and by being mostly ignorant of the
potential consequences, they opened a spiritual door that
should have remained shut. Their allegiance to the Lord es-
caped while their affinity to paganism gained entry. Then,
when a time came for them to go completely into apostasy,
the transition, while it may have been awkward at first, was
altogether easy. The church today could learn from their mis-
takes.

> My people are destroyed for lack of knowledge: because
> thou hast rejected knowledge, I will also reject thee, that
> thou shalt be no priest to me: seeing thou hast forgotten
> the law of thy God, I will also forget thy children.
>
> —Hosea 4:6

Ahab the Apostate King Marries Jezebel

Thirty-four years passed from the death of Jeroboam, the son
of Nebat, the man which made Israel to sin, until the arrival
of King Ahab to the throne of the northern kingdom. The practices that had typified the paganism of Babylon continued to
infiltrate the cultures that prevailed throughout the eastern
Mediterranean. From Asia Minor, through Phoenicia (modern Lebanon), down the coast through Israel and what later
became Gaza, then on to Egypt, the archaeologist today can
readily trace the evidence of those visible elements that accompanied Babylonian forms of worship. Signs of the zodiac
are prominent throughout the land of Israel, figurines and
icons emerge from beneath the sands and stone walls of ancient and long defunct civilizations. Temples built to accom-
modate gods and goddesses whose names often trace back to
Nimrod of Babel—Semiramis, Tammuz, Osiris, Isis, Horus,
and a host of others—continue to yield their remains to the
spade and trowel of modern scholarship. Pyramids, ziggu-

rats, obelisks, and other monuments to otherwise forgotten deities dot the landscape and testify to the amazing power these ornaments held over their people.

With the arrival of Ahab upon the throne of the ten northern tribes of Israel, known otherwise as the land of Ephraim, came the arrival of an additional influence for evil. She was Jezebel—Ahab's wife—but, more significantly, the daughter of a direct descendent of Hiram whose name was Ethbaal, king of the Sidonians.

> And it came to pass, as if it had been a light thing for him to walk in the sins of Jeroboam the son of Nebat, that he took to wife Jezebel the daughter of Ethbaal king of the Zidonians, and went and served Baal, and worshipped him.
> —1 Kings 16:31

Ahab was the son of King Omri, who evidently arranged the marriage of Ahab to a Phoenician princess for political reasons. While said marriage may have been advantageous for Omri and for Ethbaal, it proved disastrous for Israel. Adding authenticity to Baal worship by connecting it to the royal family of the north made its open practice more acceptable throughout the land.

Jezebel, whose personal name likely means "Baal is the prince," attempted to destroy God's prophets in Israel while installing the prophets of Baal and Asherah as part of the household of royalty. Upon their ignominious defeat on Mount Carmel, Jezebel threatened to kill Elijah, the prophet of God (1 Kings 19:2). Elijah, although victorious over the four hundred and fifty prophets, fled for his life from the purview of Queen Jezebel.

Jehu's Reforms

Reform eventually came to the northern kingdom, only about twelve years after the death of Ahab. The reform had its limitations, and it failed in many ways; nevertheless, Jehu, who was either a son or a grandson of military officer named Nimshi under Ahab, came to power in 841 B.C. and reigned some twenty-eight years. During this time, Jehu made some remarkable progress toward correcting the idolatrous excesses of royalty.

And Jehu gathered all the people together, and said unto them, Ahab served Baal a little; but Jehu shall serve him much. Now therefore call unto me all the prophets of Baal, all his servants, and all his priests; let none be wanting: for I have a great sacrifice to do to Baal; whosoever shall be wanting, he shall not live. But Jehu did it in subtilty, to the intent that he might destroy the worshippers of Baal. And Jehu said, Proclaim a solemn assembly for Baal. And they proclaimed it. And Jehu sent through all Israel: and all the worshippers of Baal came, so that there was not a man left that came not. And they came into the house of Baal; and the house of Baal was full from one end to another. And he said unto him that was over the vestry, Bring forth vestments for all the worshippers of Baal. And he brought them forth vestments. And Jehu went, and Jehonadab the son of Rechab, into the house of Baal, and said unto the worshippers of Baal, Search, and look that there be here with you none of the servants of the LORD, but the worshippers of Baal only. And when they went in to offer sacrifices and burnt offerings, Jehu appointed fourscore men without, and said, If any of the men whom I have brought into your hands escape, he that letteth him go, his life shall be for the life of him. And it came to pass, as soon as he had made an end of offering the burnt offering, that Jehu said to the guard and to the captains, Go in, and slay them; let none come forth. And they smote them with the edge of the sword; and the guard and the captains cast them out, and went to the city of the house of Baal. And they brought forth the images out of the house of Baal, and burned them. And they brake down the image of Baal, and brake down the house of Baal, and made it a draught house unto this day. Thus Jehu destroyed Baal out of Israel. Howbeit from the sins of Jeroboam the son of Nebat, who made Israel to sin, Jehu departed not from after them, to wit, the golden calves that were in Bethel, and that were in Dan.

—2 Kings 10:18–29

The golden calves at Dan and Bethel remained untouched by Jehu's reforms. He managed to rid the royal house of Baal worship, but left a similar blight unscathed. He might have opened a door of opportunity for reconciliation between the north and the south and made the resumption of worship at Jerusalem possible for his people. Nevertheless, he continued in the ways of Jeroboam who preceded him by ninety years. Jeroboam had been dead seventy years by the time Jehu came upon the scene, but his influence upon the younger king prevailed.

And the LORD said unto Jehu, Because thou hast done well in executing that which is right in mine eyes, and hast done unto the house of Ahab according to all that was in mine heart, thy children of the fourth generation shall sit on the throne of Israel. But Jehu took no heed to walk in the law of the LORD God of Israel with all his heart: for he departed not from the sins of Jeroboam, which made Israel to sin.

—2 Kings 10:30–31

Reform in the Southern Kingdom

Judah, the southern kingdom whose capitol was in Jerusalem, did not escape the ravages and excesses of Babylonianism. As apostasy increased and unregenerate kings came to power, as the priesthood diminished in influence and zeal, and as the Mosaic covenant suffered increasing violations and ignorance, the House of the Lord in Jerusalem suffered spiritual adultery of the basest sort.

It all had begun at the very beginning of the divided monarchy with Rehoboam, son of Solomon, on the throne in Jerusalem.

> And Judah did evil in the sight of the LORD, and they provoked him to jealousy with their sins which they had committed, above all that their fathers had done. For they also built them high places, and images, and groves, on every high hill, and under every green tree. And there were also sodomites in the land: and they did according to all the abominations of the nations which the LORD cast out before the children of Israel.
>
> —1 Kings 14:22–24

Among the various pagan religious practices condoned in Judah was male homosexual prostitution. Such practice stands universally condemned in Scripture as the ultimate distortion of mind and nature (cf. Lev. 18:22; 20:13; Rom. 1:24–32; 1 Cor. 6:9). How odd, therefore, that this violation of what is natural is a primary component of nature worship both then and now! Worship of the creature at the expense of the Creator seems to generate perverse, unnatural practices. The reprobate mind of which Paul speaks in Romans chapter one, is particularly susceptible to the exchange of the natural use of the body for that which is against nature. Exchange the truth of God for a lie, and the other exchange invariably follows. As the influence of pantheism mounts here in the twenty-first century, a concomitant rise in homosexual behavior also rises.

The Reign of King Asa
In the year 911 B.C., Asa assumed the throne as the third king

of the southern kingdom.

> And Asa did that which was right in the eyes of the Lord, as
> did David his father. And he took away the sodomites out of
> the land, and removed all the idols that his fathers had made.
> And also Maachah his mother, even her he removed from
> being queen, because she had made an idol in a grove; and
> Asa destroyed her idol, and burnt it by the brook Kidron.
> But the high places were not removed: nevertheless Asa's
> heart was perfect with the Lord all his days. And he brought
> in the things which his father had dedicated, and the things
> which himself had dedicated, into the house of the Lord,
> silver, and gold, and vessels.
>
> —1 Kings 15:11–15

According to my *Holman Bible Dictionary,* a high place as
mentioned in verse fourteen was usually upon a mountain or
hill and constituted a Canaanite place of worship.

> The average high place would have an altar (2 Kings 21:3;
> 2 Chron. 14:3), a carved wooden pole that depicted the fe-
> male goddess of fertility (Asherah), a stone pillar symboliz-
> ing the male deity [perhaps an obelisk] (2 Kings 3:2), other
> idols (2 Kings 17:29; 2 Chron. 33:19), and some type of
> building (1 Kings 12:31; 13:32; 16:32–33). At these places
> of worship the people sacrificed animals (at some high plac-
> es children were sacrificed according to Jer. 7:31), burned
> incense to their gods, prayed, ate sacrificial meals, and were
> involved with male or female cultic prostitutes (2 Kings
> 17:8–12; 21:3–7; Hos. 4:11–14). Although most high places
> were part of the worship of Baal, the Ammonite god Molech
> and the Moabite god Chemosh were also worshiped at sim-
> ilar high places (1 Kings 11:5–8; 2 Kings 23:10). Scripture
> speaks negatively about these heathen places of worship;
> still they played a central role in the lives of most of the

people who lived in Palestine before the land was defeated by Joshua. Archaeologists have discovered the remains of high places at Megiddo, Gezer, and numerous other sites.

When the Israelites came into the land of Canaan, they were ordered to destroy the high places of the people who lived in the land (Exod. 23:24; 34:13; Num. 33:52; Deut. 7:5; 12:3) lest the Israelites be tempted to worship the Canaanite false gods and accept their immoral behavior. The Israelites were to worship God at the tabernacle at Shiloh (Josh 18:1; 1 Sam. 1:3).

The Israelite prophets also condemned the high places of Moab (Isa. 15:2; 16:12), Judah (Jer. 7:30–31; 17:1–3; 19:3–5; 32:35), and Israel (Ezek. 6:3,6; 20:29–31; Hos. 10:8, Amos 7:9) because they were places of sin where false gods were worshiped.

Inescapable is the connection between sodomy and idolatry. The mind that rejects the absolute authority of God embraces sin. One of the prophesied characteristics of the age in which we live is the heart filled with inordinate affection (Rom. 1:31; 2 Tim. 3:3). Both the return to Babylonianism and the relative prominence of homosexuality characterize our day. As it was then, so is it now.

Good King Jehoshaphat

While Jehoshaphat reigned in Judah, the southern kingdom, from 870 to 848 B.C., Ahab reigned in the north with his wife, Jezebel. While the north was allowing Baal worship to proliferate, the south was ousting it from the environs of the Jerusalem Temple.

Of Jehoshaphat, the Bible says:

And he walked in all the ways of Asa his father; he turned not aside from it, doing that which was right in the eyes of the Lord: nevertheless the high places were not taken away;

for the people offered and burnt incense yet in the high places. . . . And the remnant of the sodomites, which remained in the days of his father Asa, he took out of the land.

—1 Kings 22:43, 46

Note that the people of Judah committed idolatry in the high places about them. The book of Second Chronicles makes this additional but significant comment in its account of good King Jehoshaphat: "Howbeit the high places were not taken away: for as yet the people had not prepared their hearts unto the God of their fathers" (2 Chron. 20:33).

Johoada, the Priest

The southern kingdom had other reformers who occasionally arose to cleanse the land of its whoredoms. One such reformer was the priest Jehoida. It was he who had been responsible, in collusion with Aunt Jehosheba, for the preservation of little King Joash. Grandmother Athaliah had seized the throne after the death of her son, Ahaziah, by killing all the boys in the family. She missed one. Jehosheba and Jehoida hid Joash until he was seven years old. Meanwhile, Athaliah reigned over the southern kingdom for six years, not realizing that the real king was preserved alive.

Coronation Day came with Jehoida presiding:
And he brought forth the king's son, and put the crown upon him, and gave him the testimony; and they made him king, and anointed him; and they clapped their hands, and said, God save the king.

—2 Kings 11:12

The commotion came to Athaliah's attention whereupon she cried, "Treason! Treason!" Those may have been her final words. They took her from the House of the Lord into the street where she died by the sword.

Jehoida immediately began to make a clean path for his young king who would reign in Jerusalem for the next forty years:

> And Jehoiada made a covenant between the LORD and the king and the people, that they should be the LORD's people; between the king also and the people. And all the people of the land went into the house of Baal, and brake it down; his altars and his images brake they in pieces thoroughly, and slew Mattan the priest of Baal before the altars. And the priest appointed officers over the house of the LORD.
>
> —2 Kings 11:17–18

Hezekiah, One of Judah's Great Kings

Another great reformer came about one hundred years later in the person of King Hezekiah. He was a coregent with his father, Ahaz, until the elder died. Hezekiah reigned twenty-nine years and walked in the ways of the Lord.

> And he did that which was right in the sight of the LORD, according to all that David his father did. He removed the high places, and brake the images, and cut down the groves, and brake in pieces the brasen serpent that Moses had made: for unto those days the children of Israel did burn incense to it: and he called it Nehushtan.
>
> —2 Kings 18:3–4

Hezekiah had a "no tolerance" policy for paganism. He even destroyed the brazen serpent that Moses had erected in the wilderness wanderings nearly eight centuries earlier. The pole had become a "holy grail" of its day, a relic that had inspired cultic worship among some of the people.

He trusted in the LORD God of Israel; so that after him was none like him among all the kings of Judah, nor any that were before him. For he clave to the LORD, and departed not from following him, but kept his commandments, which the LORD commanded Moses.

—2 Kings 18:5–6

Hezekiah's reforms as recorded in Second Chronicles 29:3–31:21 constitute the most extensive and successful revival in biblical history with the possible exception of the Day of Pentecost. The exposition of it all is beyond the scope of this presentation, but the study of it is rewarding and inspiring.

Josiah's Reforms

The next reformer and the last of the spiritually successful kings in the southern kingdom is Josiah:

And the king went up into the house of the LORD, and all the men of Judah and all the inhabitants of Jerusalem with him, and the priests, and the prophets, and all the people, both small and great: and he read in their ears all the words of the book of the covenant which was found in the house of the LORD.

—2 Kings 23:2

Most scholars agree that the book of the covenant here was a portion of the Pentateuch, rather than its entirety—perhaps Deuteronomy chapters twenty-seven and twenty-eight describing either the blessings for obedience to the Mosaic covenant or the discipline for disobedience. How marvelous when the king will take the spiritual initiative and lead his nation in repentance and in submission to the Word of God.

And the king stood by a pillar, and made a covenant before the LORD, to walk after the LORD, and to keep his commandments and his testimonies and his statutes with all their heart and all their soul, to perform the words of this covenant that were written in this book. And all the people stood to the covenant.

—2 Kings 23:3

A repentant people recognized their failure to meet the standards and requirements of the Law. With their worthy leader, Josiah, they pledged their loyalty to the commandments of God.

And the king commanded Hilkiah the high priest, and the priests of the second order, and the keepers of the door, to bring forth out of the temple of the LORD all the vessels that were made for Baal, and for the grove, and for all the host of heaven: and he burned them without Jerusalem in the fields of Kidron, and carried the ashes of them unto Bethel. And he put down the idolatrous priests, whom the kings of Judah had ordained to burn incense in the high places in the cities of Judah, and in the places round about Jerusalem; them also that burned incense unto Baal, to the sun, and to the moon, and to the planets, and to all the host of heaven.

—2 Kings 23:4–5

References to the celestial bodies suggest several forms of occult and false religious practices. First, the sun god speaks of the Egyptian god, Ra, and of the exalted Nimrod and Osiris. Additionally, the burning of incense speaks of worshiping both the celestial bodies and the gods and goddesses representing them—including the infamous Ishtar, moon goddess of Ur of the Chaldees. In addition, the occult practice of astrology comes to mind as these heavenly orbs and stars receive homage from people whose allegiance was to have been to the Lord exclusively.

And he brought out the grove from the house of the LORD, without Jerusalem, unto the brook Kidron, and burned it at the brook Kidron, and stamped it small to powder, and cast the powder thereof upon the graves of the children of the people.

—2 Kings 23:6

The "grove" (Heb. *asherah*) is a wooden pole fashioned into a figure before which men and women bow and commit sacrilege. Invariably, these could be found in the "high places" of pagan worship, likely representing the female deities worshiped there. Israel seemed to be well-endowed with these idols because the apostasy at this stage of Israel's history was thoroughly entrenched and widespread. This object cited in Second Kings 23:6 rested in the Jerusalem Temple until Josiah and company removed it.

Later in Israel's history, and against the will of her leaders and their people, a comparable abomination took place as a Syrian leader emerged known as Antiochus IV Epiphanes. He committed the original Abomination of Desolation by sacrificing a pig on the sacred altar of the Temple and by erecting an image of the pagan god Zeus in the Most Holy Place.

An equally ugly figure will emerge during the Tribulation period who will desecrate the Temple (not yet built, but prophetic) in similar fashion. Jesus spoke of this in Matthew 24:15, declaring that this fulfillment is yet future.

And he brake down the houses of the sodomites, that were by the house of the LORD, where the women wove hangings for the grove.

—2 Kings 23:7

Again we note the proximity of homosexuals (male prostitutes) to the religious center and associated with paganism.

The homosexuals lived and performed their "religious duties" in close vicinity to the Jerusalem Temple. Nearby, perhaps associated with the sodomites, women worked making coverings for the female deity or idol inside the Temple.

> And he brought all the priests out of the cities of Judah, and defiled the high places where the priests had burned incense, from Geba to Beersheba, and brake down the high places of the gates that were in the entering in of the gate of Joshua the governor of the city, which were on a man's left hand at the gate of the city. Nevertheless the priests of the high places came not up to the altar of the LORD in Jerusalem, but they did eat of the unleavened bread among their brethren. And he defiled Topheth, which is in the valley of the children of Hinnom, that no man might make his son or his daughter to pass through the fire to Molech.
>
> —2 Kings 23:8–10

Molech was a metallic idol erected in the outskirts of the Holy City which received the sacrifice of small children. The idol was heated to a red-hot state, then living children were placed in its glowing arms to be consumed, cooked alive, by the intense heat.

> And he took away the horses that the kings of Judah had given to the sun, at the entering in of the house of the LORD, by the chamber of Nathanmelech the chamberlain, which was in the suburbs, and burned the chariots of the sun with fire. And the altars that were on the top of the upper chamber of Ahaz, which the kings of Judah had made, and the altars which Manasseh had made in the two courts of the house of the LORD, did the king beat down, and brake them down from thence, and cast the dust of them into the brook Kidron. And the high places that were before Jerusalem, which were on the right hand of the mount of corruption,

which Solomon the king of Israel had builded for Ashtoreth the abomination of the Zidonians, and for Chemosh the abomination of the Moabites, and for Milcom the abomination of the children of Ammon, did the king defile. And he brake in pieces the images, and cut down the groves, and filled their places with the bones of men. Moreover the altar that was at Bethel, and the high place which Jeroboam the son of Nebat, who made Israel to sin, had made, both that altar and the high place he brake down, and burned the high place, and stamped it small to powder, and burned the grove.

—2 Kings 23:11–15

Josiah even went north into the northern kingdom and destroyed the pagan centers of worship in the land of King Jeroboam.

And as Josiah turned himself, he spied the sepulchres that were there in the mount, and sent, and took the bones out of the sepulchres, and burned them upon the altar, and polluted it, according to the word of the LORD which the man of God proclaimed, who proclaimed these words.

—2 Kings 23:16

In fulfillment of the prophecy brought to Jeroboam I by the "man of God" over three hundred years before, Josiah burned the bones of the false priests on the altar which Jeroboam had erected, and then he destroyed the altar and its high place (cf. 1 Kings 13:1–3).

And all the houses also of the high places that were in the cities of Samaria, which the kings of Israel had made to provoke the LORD to anger, Josiah took away, and did to them according to all the acts that he had done in Bethel.

And he slew all the priests of the high places that were there upon the altars, and burned men's bones upon them, and returned to Jerusalem. And the king commanded all the people, saying, Keep the passover unto the LORD your God, as it is written in the book of this covenant.

—2 Kings 23:19–21

This is a sad commentary on the spiritual life of God's ancient people. As a nation, they only celebrated the Passover for a few years, into the time of the judges, and prior to the reign of the monarchs, Saul, David, and Solomon. Now, some four hundred years had passed during which the Passover, so sacred as it was, had been neglected. How patient the Lord had been; how derelict His people!

Surely there was not holden such a passover from the days of the judges that judged Israel, nor in all the days of the kings of Israel, nor of the kings of Judah; But in the eighteenth year of king Josiah, wherein this passover was holden to the LORD in Jerusalem.

—2 Kings 23:22–23

Thank the Lord for good King Josiah. His revival lasted but a short time, but the record of it in Scripture reminds us of God's mercy and grace. It also reminds us that even in a period of utter declension, revival can occur among His people and that God will move and save even when men and women seem to have forsaken Him for long and empty periods of time.

Next, the occult workers came under the wrath of God as administered by His servant, Josiah.

Moreover the workers with familiar spirits, and the wizards, and the images, and the idols, and all the abominations that were spied in the land of Judah and in Jerusa lem, did Josiah put away, that he might perform the words of the law which were written in the book that Hilkiah the priest found in the house of the LORD. And like unto him was there no king before him, that turned to the LORD with all his heart, and with all his soul, and with all his might, according to all the law of Moses; neither after him arose there any like him.

—2 Kings 23:24–25

This verse classifies Josiah as one of the greatest kings of Judah because he tried to bring Judah back to God. How unfortunate that many world leaders today make an unusual effort to lead people away from the truth and back into the falsehood of paganism.

Both Israel in the north, and Judah in the south experienced the awesome discipline of God. By 722 B.C., the northern kingdom faced captivity at the hands of the Assyrian Empire, and one hundred sixteen years later, Babylon took the southern kingdom into captivity.

The indictment of God in both cases was much the same. For the north:

Israel Carried Captive to Assyria

Then the king of Assyria came up throughout all the land, and went up to Samaria, and besieged it three years. In the ninth year of Hoshea the king of Assyria took Samaria, and carried Israel away into Assyria, and placed them in Halah and in Habor by the river of Gozan, and in the cities of the Medes.

—2 Kings 17:5–6

After three years of siege, Samaria fell to the Assyrians, and the days of Israel as a sovereign power were over (2 Kings 18:10). Many of the Israelites were taken captive and deported to Assyrian cities (vs. 23; 18:11). Sargon II (722–705 B.C.), who succeeded Shalmaneser V, took credit for the victory and boasted that he carried away 27,290 people from Samaria. Some claim that the ten northern tribes became "lost" at this time, but only a relatively few people of the hundreds of thousands living in the north actually made the forcible trek into the land of their enemy. The kingdom as a sovereign power became "lost," but the tribes themselves never disappeared.

> For so it was, that the children of Israel had sinned against the Lord their God, which had brought them up out of the land of Egypt, from under the hand of Pharaoh king of Egypt, and had feared other gods, And walked in the statutes of the heathen, whom the Lord cast out from before the children of Israel, and of the kings of Israel, which they had made. And the children of Israel did secretly those things that were not right against the Lord their God, and they built them high places in all their cities, from the tower of the watchmen to the fenced city. And they set them up images and groves in every high hill, and under every green tree.
>
> —2 Kings 17:7–10

One of my commentaries makes the following entry on verse ten:

> From the time they settled in Canaan until the Exile, Israel was influenced by its idolatrous neighbors. These influences were aided by mixed marriages, such as those of Solomon (1 Kings 11:1–13) and Ahab (1 Kings 16:30–33), and by the popular belief that the local gods of Canaan exercised proprietorship (vss. 7–12).

> And there they burnt incense in all the high places, as did the heathen whom the Lord carried away before them; and

wrought wicked things to provoke the LORD to anger: For they served idols, whereof the LORD had said unto them, Ye shall not do this thing. Yet the LORD testified against Israel, and against Judah, by all the prophets, and by all the seers, saying, Turn ye from your evil ways, and keep my commandments and my statutes, according to all the law which I commanded your fathers, and which I sent to you by my servants the prophets. Notwithstanding they would not hear, but hardened their necks, like to the neck of their fathers, that did not believe in the LORD their God. And they rejected his statutes, and his covenant that he made with their fathers, and his testimonies which he testified against them; and they followed vanity, and became vain, and went after the heathen that were round about them, concerning whom the LORD had charged them, that they should not do like them. And they left all the commandments of the LORD their God, and made them molten images, even two calves, and made a grove, and worshipped all the host of heaven, and served Baal. And they caused their sons and their daughters to pass through the fire, and used divination and enchantments, and sold themselves to do evil in the sight of the LORD, to provoke him to anger. Therefore the LORD was very angry with Israel, and removed them out of his sight: there was none left but the tribe of Judah only.

—2 Kings 17:11–18

If Jesus Christ is the same yesterday, today, and forever (Heb. 13:8) then we can assume that those practices that made Him angry at Israel as indicated above, continue to make Him angry today. The captivity of an entire nation was the direct result of dabbling with the occult, with idols, and the pagan deities that all proliferated both within and along the borders of this northern kingdom.

Then, of the southern kingdom's captivity we read:

Moreover all the chief of the priests, and the people, transgressed very much after all the abominations of the heathen; and polluted the house of the LORD which he had hallowed in Jerusalem.

—2 Chronicles 36:14

In keeping with his purpose, the chronicler provides the reason for the Babylonian captivity: it resulted from the apostasy, idolatry, and arrogance of the people when they were confronted by God's messengers (cf. Jer. 25:11–12).

If you think God neither cares about nor notices your annual veneration of evergreen trees, hiding Easter (Ishtar) eggs, fondness for figurines, trinkets, and other icons, or your celebration of a satanic witch's holiday, etc., you might want to rethink your position. He found no favor with people centuries ago who should have known better. Our "enlightened" generation is even more culpable than they.

Chapter Four

Halloween:
The Occult Connection

Some people find the negative in everything! Bible preachers of the past warned people of Hollywood's excesses and its conveyance of immoral values. Prognosticators of doom warned of a New World Order, a global economy, and a New Age religion. Alarmists saw danger lurking around every corner and doom on every horizon. They saw the Devil in everything they considered disagreeable. They were able to outshine Chicken Little—hands down.

This enlightened generation now rests perfectly safe in the knowledge the sky is not about to fall. But all those other disturbing predictions are bearing fruit. We've been warned not to trifle with the occult. We've heard frightful stories about Ouija boards, tarot cards, and altered states of consciousness. Nevertheless, each October 31 we dabble with the occult and the satanic. Even worse, adults annually foist this flirtation with evil upon their children. And although thousands of young people become entrapped each year by Satanism, cults, the drug culture, spiritism, necromancy, and other forms of divination and occult practices, parents continue to ridicule those Chicken Little-types who insist that trifling with the occult is unhealthy, unwise, and ungodly.

Children do not necessarily embrace other practices that are sinister, evil, and demonic just because they dress up in a costume for Halloween. A child parading down a street in costume, playing trick or treat, or soaping somebody's window may not automatically become a candidate for witchcraft, demon possession, or the metaphysical. Nevertheless, the celebration of Halloween by children makes them less sensitive to the dangers of experimenting with the occult. Witches lose their repulsiveness, communicating with the dead seems less horrifying, and demonic entities less threatening when they become familiar. Especially is this true when the person behind the mask turns out to be a friend or neighbor—not a fiend after all. Then, when parents make light of these activities and personages, children begin to lose any sense of fear or trepidation of such beings. Furthermore, beliefs and practices associated with them likewise seem more tolerable. In other words, Halloween forms a link with occult activities and personages. It is important to realize that the occult connection is dangerous and, in a Christian context, intolerable.

Halloween Practices in Ancient Times

The word *occult* means "hidden." Included in a catalog of occult practices are the following: divination, astrology, spiritualism, numerology, yoga, demonology, divining with rod or pendulum, and numerous other, related practices. They are occult because they are hidden; they are hidden because they thrive on their "mystery" nature. In addition, they are forbidden by Scripture, and for centuries the church has limited them to covert practices.

In his book *A History of Magic, Witchcraft and Occultism*, W. B. Crow includes the Feast of Samhain among those occult festivals celebrated annually in antiquity. That festival, originating among the Druids of the Celtic tribes of Britain, France, and northern Europe, became absorbed by the Roman Catholic Church and titled "All Saints (Hallows) Day." It was celebrated each November 1, but the evening before became known as All Hallow E'en. For the Celts, this was the end of one year and the first day of the next. In addition, it marked the passage from a season of growth, harvest, and warmth, to one of death, darkness, and cold.

To celebrate this annual and seasonal passage, the Druids built huge bonfires. These fires served double duty: they warded off demons and such which roamed around, but they also provided for a sacrifice to the sun god. In enormous wicker baskets, they caged both human and animal sacrifices and burned their victims alive. By observing the way they died, the priests predicted good or evil for the future.

Later in the new year, when the sun began a northward trek in the sky, and days began to grow longer again, they celebrated the winter solstice with the burning of the Yule log. Since the sun had reversed itself and was now rising higher in the sky, it indicated the sun god's acceptance of the sacrifices of Samhain. This celebration took place at the time of our Christmas celebration and, like other pagan practices, became absorbed by or syncretized with it. We continue to "Deck the halls with boughs of holly; troll the ancient yuletide carol," and "See the blazing yule before us. Fa la la la la la la la la." Although the song and the practice are clearly pagan, they are an integral part of what we celebrate as Christmas.

Each October 31, Samhain, lord of the dead, supposedly assembled the souls of all those who had died during the previous year. The spirits of the dead left their graves and roamed the earth or visited their former homes and families.

This was the vigil of Samhain. To pay for their sins, these souls were put into the bodies of animals. The greater the person's sins, the lower the animal into which his or her soul was placed. All sorts of goblins, spirits, and fairies were thought to roam the earth during the vigil of Samhain.

—D. J. Herda, *Halloween*, pp. 1–2

In addition to burning people (including children) alive, the Celts performed other rituals,

. . . for the sake of their safety and well-being. People put out sweets and other good things to eat to placate the evil spirits and keep them from doing harm. Some people, hoping to fool the demons, disguised themselves as evil spirits and roamed the countryside, committing malicious pranks, until dawn sent the ghosts and devils back to their unholy realm.

—Peter R. Limburg, *Weird! The Complete Book of Halloween Words*, p. 5

In an October 1984 publication of the *Gospel Truth*, Bill Uselton documents that the people left only the best mutton legs, vegetables, eggs, and poultry—as well as honey and wine—outside for the spirits to consume on their way to the netherworld. Failure to treat the evil ones might result in their intrusion upon one's house and its belongings. The game of "trick or treat" is more than two thousand years old.

The ancient practice of "wassailing" derived from what is now the celebration of Halloween. By A.D. 50 the Romans had invaded both Britain and Gaul (France) and had brought their traditions with them. Among them was the Feast of Pomona. It was held at the same time as Samhain and the two celebrations eventually merged.

[Pomona] honored their harvest goddess of the same name. Fruits, especially apples, were sacred to Pomona. Many Halloween customs and games that feature apples, apple peelings, or nuts, probably date from this time.

—Cass R. Sandak, Halloween, pp. 9–10

The Romans pictured Pomona as a beautiful young maiden, her arms filled with fruit, and a crown of apples on her head. To thank Pomona for good harvests, the Romans laid out apples and nuts in her honor. Then they played various games, held races, and celebrated throughout the day and night.

—D. J. Herda, Halloween, p. 2

[Today] in some apple-growing districts, such as Devon and Somerset, it is still the custom to hold special ceremonies each winter to encourage the growth of apples in the coming year. They call these ceremonies "Wassailing parties." The wassailers go into the orchards and drink to the health of every tree. Then everyone throws part of the drink, followed by stones or even gunshot, through the bare branches of the trees. It was once thought that this would drive out any evil spirits in the orchard.

—Roderick Hunt, Ghosts, Witches, and
Things Like That, p. 27

An additional Roman festival for the dead, Fernalia, became mingled with Pomona and Samhain. With a few added embellishments, these pagan and occult activities became Halloween as we know it today.

The Church Embraces Halloween

As Christianity spread throughout Europe, the church sought to eliminate the pagan practices of the Celts by giving the

Samhain and Fernalia a new meaning. Most cultures set aside a day for remembering their dead, so the Roman church designated November 1 as All Hallows Day to eulogize departed saints. The church first recognized this holiday in A.D. 837 (Sandak, p. 11). On November 2, they observed All Souls Day to commemorate those departed ones who were *not* saints. The church struggled in vain to eliminate the heathenism inherent in the celebrations. To the church's chagrin, it spawned instead an organized cult opposed to the church—witchcraft.

> Halloween became known as the "night of the witch." It was then, according to superstition, that the devil and all of his followers—witches, warlocks, and demons—gathered. They would mock the coming of the church's festival of All Saints Day on November 1 by performing unholy acts.
>
> —D. J. Herda, *Halloween*, p. 2

Edna Barth, in her book *Witches, Pumpkins and Grinning Ghosts*, describes Halloween as one of four sabbaths celebrated annually by witches in Europe:

> The sabbaths were joyful, and people looked forward to them. Sometimes thousands attended. Among them were members of noble or royal families, their faces concealed by masks.
>
> The assembled witches vowed to obey their god, the master disguised as an animal. They kissed him on whatever part of his body he chose and paid homage by turning "widdershins"—from east to west—a certain number of times. They pledged their children to the god and thanked him as the source of food and of life itself.
>
> At Halloween sabbaths witches did dances to make animals more fertile, dressing up like animals themselves. To encourage fertility in human beings, they danced naked or in their usual clothes. In some of the dances they galloped

about straddling branches or broomsticks.

As they danced, the witches chanted. Before long, the rhythmic movements, the rhythmic sounds, and the feeling of being at one with their horned god gave them a sense of ecstasy.

Some witches had been born into the religion. Others, including many learned men, were attracted by the magic practices. Still others joined in resentment against the Christian church. To a downtrodden peasant, the excitement of the witch cult had more appeal than the droning services held at church.

Many who joined were women. Few members of their sex had any status then. All were looked on as men's inferiors. Almost all were little more than their husband's property. In the witch cult, they found equality.

For most people of the time—overworked and underfed—life was bleak. So they reached toward anything, like the witch cult, that promised release and joy.

Accoutrements of Halloween

Associated with witches on holiday cards, decorations, and the accoutrements of Halloween are owls, bats, cats, and toads. Their significance must not be overlooked. They are an important link between Halloween and the occult. They are known as "the witch's familiars."

A *divining familiar* was the species of animal whose shape the "Devil" would take to help the witch in divining the future. A witch trying to find out the length of a person's life or of an illness would watch the familiar closely. The speed or slowness of the animal's movements, the direction in which it moved, the kinds of sounds it made—all these were considered clues.

—Edna Barth, Witches, *Pumpkins, and Grinning Ghosts*, p. 43

Other familiars listed include hens, geese, small dogs, rats, or even butterflies, wasps, crickets, and snails. These creatures were considered demon controlled and the manifestation of what the Bible terms a "familiar spirit." Paul, the apostle, confronted a girl bewitched by such a spirit on the streets of Phillipi:

> And it came to pass, as we went to prayer, a certain damsel possessed with a spirit of divination met us, which brought her masters much gain by soothsaying: The same followed Paul and us, and cried, saying, These men are the servants of the most high God, which shew unto us the way of salvation. And this did she many days. But Paul, being grieved, turned and said to the spirit, I command thee in the name of Jesus Christ to come out of her. And he came out the same hour.
>
> —Acts, 16:16–18

Consequently, any contact with such "familiar spirits" is a matter of serious concern.

Note carefully that Paul did not treat the situation lightly, nor did he regard it as silly superstition or fiction. Scripture ascribes similar gravity to the subject in other passages:

> Thou shalt not suffer a witch to live.
>
> —Exod. 22:18

> Regard not them that have familiar spirits, neither seek after wizards, to be defiled by them: I am the Lord your God.
>
> —Lev. 19:31

> A man also or woman that hath a familiar spirit, or that is a wizard, shall surely be put to death: they shall stone them with stones: their blood shall be upon them.
>
> —Lev. 20:27

Halloween decorations of every sort abound with the emblems of these *familiars* and witches that accompany them. They are satanic, occult, and forbidden by Scripture.

Inquisitions

Witch hunts began relatively early in medieval times. By 1163, Pope Alexander III asked the Council of Tours to condemn the Manichean cults proliferating in parts of Europe. The Third Lateran Council in 1179 also investigated heretics, and by 1184 Lucius III named some of them in a papal bull. The moves against false religions were gaining acceptability.

> By 1235, the term "Inquisition" was being freely used. On December 13, 1248, Pope Alexander IV addressed his papal bull against witchcraft to the Franciscan Inquisitors. In 1330 a witch was burned in southern France. Over the next twenty years some six hundred people were sent to the stake for heresy or witchcraft.
> —Roger C. Palms, *The Christian and the Occult,* p. 40

Popes took increasingly stronger measures against witchcraft throughout the fourteenth and fifteenth centuries. In 1429, Joan of Arc, a shepherdess who led the French in battle claiming that angels spoke to her, was burned at the stake for witchcraft. As long as they were winning, the French had no objection to her beliefs. But when the French began to lose in battle, they turned against her. She died at the stake in the town square of Rouen (Sandak, p. 17).

"In 1487, a book titled *Hammer of Witches* was published by two European witch-hunters. It became the manual for Inquisitors" (Palms, p. 40). In 1484, Pope Innocent VIII pronounced an edict outlawing Samhain and the witchcraft that accompanied it. Witches continued to meet covertly, wearing dark clothing, and congregating in forests and fields. They wore cone-shaped hats that were simply the fashion of that day. The pope's pronouncement perpetuated the witch hunts that continued through A.D. 1750. Hundreds of people were tortured, executed, and their bodies burned and desecrated; nevertheless, witchcraft continued and it proliferates to this day. In the United States, an organization called *Wicca* (wise woman) boasts membership of between two hundred thousand and five hundred thousand witches and warlocks.

Of the eight major festivals celebrated annually by witches today, Halloween is the greatest. These "wise women" continue to mix herb potions and charms in little shops. They include students, housewives, businessmen and women, and other professionals. Although some claim to be following a satanic religion, others say they only wish to go back in time to a "higher wisdom" and a primitive lifestyle. Indeed, the New Age is replete with their kind. They mix magic, astrology, and forms of fortune-telling. They recruit to themselves children and adults who see no harm in participating in the fun and games of Halloween and related activities.

Halloween in America

The American version of Halloween came from Ireland where Halloween is still a national holiday. The potato famine in 1840 brought thousands of immigrants from the Emerald Isle. With them came the goblins, jack o'lanterns, bonfires, apples, nuts, and pranks.

Before treats became part of Halloween, "little goblins" hid any movable thing they could find. Many a family stood guard through the night to insure their gates, outdoor furniture, or buildings would be safe. As pranks became more malicious, towns began to plan special activities. Halloween parties, costume contests, and parades gained in popularity. Giving treats became an accepted way of prevent-

ing some of the Halloween tricks. "Trick or Treat" became
the American Halloween chant.

—Jill Hierstein-Morris, *Halloween: Facts and Fun*, p. 12

The Irish are also responsible for bringing trick or treating to
great popularity in America. In Ireland on October 31 peasants went from house to house to receive offerings to their
Druid god, Muck Olla.

> This ancient procession was led by a man wearing a white
> robe and a horse head mask. (The horse was sacred, a symbol of fertility, to the Druid's sun god.) The leader was called
> Lair Bahn, which means white mare. Behind him walked
> the young men who served as his assistants, blowing cows'
> horns to let the villagers know they were coming. . . .

The procession stopped at each house to tell the farmer his
prosperity was due to the benevolence of Muck Olla. He must
now open his purse to Muck Olla, else misfortune might befall the farmer, his family, and his crops. Few farmers risked
any such displeasure of the pagan deity, so the procession
returned home with eggs, butter, corn, potatoes, and, in some
cases, coins (Herda, pp. 23–24). To the Irish farmers this was
no joke; they greatly feared that the Celtic god might destroy
their homes and barns. Without doubt, such maliciousness
was known to happen, whether Muck Olla was responsible
or not. Trick or treat is part of this pagan heritage. No matter
how "cute" their costumes, or how innocent their intentions,
contemporary goblins reenact a less-than-desirable activity
each Halloween.

In addition to the "familiars," broomsticks, and other Halloween accoutrements already considered, notice the occult
character of this emblem of the celebration: the *Jack o'Lantern*.

In the Middle Ages, Celts often hollowed out a turnip and

carved a grotesque face on it to fool demons. They carried such lanterns to light their way in the dark and to ward off evil spirits at the same time. While the turnip continues to be popular in Europe today, the pumpkin has replaced it in America. "Jack" is a nickname for "John," which is a common slang word meaning "man." Jack o'Lantern, then means, "man with a lantern."

For all these reasons, Halloween is not an acceptable holiday for Christians to celebrate. However, there is still more. In their book *Halloween and Satanism*, Phil Phillips and Joan Hake Robie list "Twelve Forbidden Practices" taken directly from the Bible. We list them here to emphasize their connections to Halloween:

1. **Enchantment**. The act of influencing by charms and incantations the practice of magical arts. *"There shall not be found among you any one that maketh his son or his daughter to pass through the fire, or that useth divination, or an observer of times, or an enchanter, or a witch, Or a charmer, or a consulter with familiar spirits, or a wizard, or a necromancer. For all that do these things are an abomination unto the Lord: and because of these abominations the Lord thy God doth drive them out from before thee"* (Deut. 18:10–12).

2. **Witchcraft**. The practice of dealing with evil spirits, the use of sorcery or magic. *"Now the works of the flesh are manifest, which are these; Adultery, fornication, uncleanness, lasciviousness, Idolatry, witchcraft . . ."* (Gal. 5:19–20).

3. **Sorcery**. The use of power gained from the assistance or control of evil spirits, especially for divining. *"But the fearful, and unbelieving, and the abominable, and murderers, and whoremongers, and sorcerers, and idolaters, and all liars, shall have their part in the lake*

which burneth with fire and brimstone: which is the second death" (Rev. 21:8).

4. **Divination**. Fortune telling. *"For thus saith the Lord of hosts, the God of Israel; Let not your prophets and your diviners, that be in the midst of you, deceive you, neither hearken to your dreams which ye cause to be dreamed. For they prophesy falsely unto you in my name: I have not sent them , saith the Lord"* (Jer. 29:8–9).

5. **Wizardry**. The art or practices of a wizard; sorcery. **Wizard**. One skilled in magic; male witch; sorcerer. *"Regard not them that have familiar spirits, neither seek after wizards, to be defiled by them: I am the Lord your God"* (Lev. 19:31).

6. **Necromancy**. Communication with the dead. Conjuring up of the spirits of the dead for purposes of magically revealing the future or influencing the course of events. *"And when they shall say unto you, Seek unto them that have familiar spirits, and unto wizards that peep, and that mutter: should not a people seek unto their God? for the living to the dead?"* (Isa. 8:19).

7. **Charm**. To put a spell upon someone; to affect by magic. *"And the spirit of Egypt shall fail in the midst thereof; and I will destroy the counsel thereof: and they shall seek to the idols, and to the charmers, and to them that have familiar spirits, and to the wizards"* (Isa. 19:3).

8. **Stargazing\astrology**. The divination of the supposed influence of the stars upon human affairs and terrestrial events by their positions and aspects. *"Thus saith the Lord, Learn not the way of the heathen, and be not dismayed at the signs of heaven; for the heathen are dismayed at them"* (Jer. 10:2).

9. **Soothsaying**. The act of foretelling events; prophesying by a spirit other than the Holy Spirit. *"And I will cut off witchcrafts out of thine hand; and thou shalt have no more soothsayers"* (Mic. 5:12).

10. **Prognostication**. To foretell from signs or symptoms; prophesying without the Holy Spirit; soothsaying. *"Stand now with thine enchantments, and with the multitude of thy sorceries, wherein thou hast labored from thy youth; if so be thou shalt be able to profit, if so be thou mayest prevail. Thou art wearied in the multitude of thy counsels. Let now the astrologers, the stargazers, the monthly prognosticators, stand up, and save thee from these things that shall come upon thee. Behold, they shall be as stubble; the fire shall burn them; they shall not deliver themselves from the power of the flame: there shall not be a coal to warm at, nor fire to sit before it. Thus shall they be unto thee with whom thou hast labored, even thy merchants, from thy youth: they shall wander every one to his quarter; none shall save thee"* (Isa. 47:12–15).

11. **Observing times.** Astrology. *"And he made his son pass through the fire, and observed times, and used enchantments, and dealt with familiar spirits and wizards: he wrought much wickedness in the sight of the Lord, to provoke him to anger"* (2 Kings 21:6).

12. **Magic**. Witchcraft. *"There shall not be found among you any one that maketh his son or his daughter to pass through the fire, or that useth divination, or an observer of times, or an enchanter, or a witch"* (Deut. 18:10).

At the risk of seeming negative and morose, we feel it best to warn you that Halloween is a point of contact with evil of every sort. Many of its roots lie in those evils specifically prohibited by the Bible. Its celebration is an affront to the faith once delivered to the saints. Halloween and Christianity are totally incompatible. To embrace the one is to frustrate the other. This brings us to an important point.

Have you ever placed your faith and trust in Jesus? His purpose in coming to earth has something to do with Halloween.

> Forasmuch then as the children are partakers of flesh and blood, he also himself likewise took part of the same; that through death he might destroy him that had the power of death, that is, the devil.
>
> —Heb. 2:14

When Jesus died on the cross, He eliminated the fear of death, which is one of the ways the Devil has entrapped people like the Celts, Druids, and others. They sought every false and ungodly way to avert death and darkness; they only needed Jesus who is the source of life and light.

Jesus paid your sin-debt by His death on a Roman cross nearly two thousand years ago. If you will accept this fact, and repent of your sins (renounce them and forsake them), you will receive right-standing with God forever. When death comes, you will instantly be in the presence of Jesus forever.

> But as many as received him, to them gave he power to become the sons of God, even to them that believe on his name.
>
> —John 1:12

Chapter Five
Vestiges of Babylonian Worship

Paganism began its rivalry with theocratic authority within a generation following the Flood. However, since vestiges of Babylonian forms of worship can be found on each continent much later in history, we must assume that by the time of Eber, Peleg, and Joktan, the various modalities of this religious system were fully entrenched.

> And Arphaxad begat Salah; and Salah begat Eber. And unto Eber were born two sons: the name of one was Peleg; for in his days was the earth divided; and his brother's name was Joktan.
>
> —Genesis 10:24–25

Eber was one of the great-grandsons of Shem. The name Eber means "beyond" or "across." Eber had a son he named Joktan, a name meaning "to make smaller." His other son he named "Peleg, for in his days was the earth divided." Combining the three names of Peleg, Joktan, and Eber, their appellations may mean that the earth was "divided into smaller regions beyond." Many Bible scholars believe that in the days of Peleg, a division of tectonic plates may have begun that resulted in the continental drift we observe today.

Both secular and religious authorities believe that the earth once consisted of a single land mass surrounded by water. Beneath the surface, however, massive continent-sized tracts began to move away from each other. That rate of motion today is infinitesimal; however, we have no way of knowing the rate at which these continents began to separate in antiquity.

The spread of Babylonian culture throughout the entire planet suggests that this spread began while the continents remained conjoined. It seems only reasonable that once the nations became separated linguistically, racially, and geographically, elements of the original religious system began to take on local or regional character and flavor. Nevertheless, the themes remained much the same. Star gazing (astrology), pursuit of the paranormal, solstice worship, and idolatry spread throughout the globe although the individual civilizations had no further contact.

Consequently, the aborigines in America had certain cultural similarities with indigenous people of other geographical locations. Inhabitants of the Pacific Islands had cultural phenomena that were similar to other people in far remote lands and places. Even if one discounts the Tower of Babel incident as mythological, or claims that the continental division must have taken place earlier in history, it is easier to account for these similarities by ascribing to them a common origin in a particular place and time than by any other hypothesis. Babel and vicinity stands the test historically, and we are satisfied that the Bible is thoroughly accurate in the matter.

By inference, we also can conclude that paganism had become fully entrenched, and had begun to supplant the worship of the Lord within three generations following the Flood. Not only did the people disobey the Lord by establishing a global society at Babel, they began a downward spiral into sin described by the apostle Paul in Romans chapter one, beginning at the nineteenth verse. It began when they exchanged the truth of God for a lie:

> Because that, when they knew God, they glorified him not as God, neither were thankful; but became vain in their imaginations, and their foolish heart was darkened. Professing themselves to be wise, they became fools, And changed the glory of the uncorruptible God into an image made like to corruptible man, and to birds, and fourfooted beasts, and creeping things.
>
> —Romans 1:21–23

> Peleg was born one hundred and one years after the Flood began. So if the paganism that originated at Babel precipitated the division of the earth into tectonic plates and drifting continents, then it must have begun its exponential growth shortly after eight people disembarked from the Ark.
>
> — *Longevity Chart: Adam to Joseph*,
> Nathan M. Meyer and Alice Hoover, 1995

"And Cush begat Nimrod: he began to be a mighty one in the earth" (Gen. 10:8). The founder of Babel, Nimrod, was a son of Cush through Ham. He was born one generation before Peleg. Because many of these early generations following the Flood seemed to be thirty years or so in length, we can assume that Nimrod was perhaps thirty years older than Peleg. Although much of this is speculation, it would seem that in just thirty years the entire pagan system of Babel had emerged to the point where only Divine intervention could have curtailed it. Noah had found grace in the eyes of the Lord and was perfect in his generations (Gen. 6:9). His grandsons and their families squandered their relationship to the Lord, exchanged the truth of God for a lie, and yielded to the world, the flesh, and the Devil practically overnight! It happened that way before; it can happen that way again. ("And as it was in the days of Noe, so shall it be also in the days of the Son of man" [Luke 17:26].)

The judgment of God fell upon the inhabitants of this globalist community at Babel, driving them to the far reaches of the earth.

> And the LORD came down to see the city and the tower, which the children of men builded. ["But the Lord came down" is sarcasm; the most magnificent efforts of men were still puny in God's eyes.] And the LORD said, Behold, the people is one, and they have all one language; and this they begin to do: and now nothing will be restrained from them, which they have imagined to do. Go to, let us go down, and there confound their language, that they may not understand one another's speech. So the LORD scattered them abroad from thence upon the face of all the earth: and they left off to build the city. Therefore is the name of it called Babel; because the LORD did there confound the language of all the earth: and from thence did the LORD scatter them abroad upon the face of all the earth.
>
> —Genesis 11:5–9

Consequently, the diffusion of pagan practices followed its adherents throughout the globe roughly 2300 B.C. At about this time, the cult of Osiris, Isis, and Horus became evident in Egyptian culture.

> Osiris, god of the dead and the underworld, was one of the most important deities in ancient Egypt. A fertility god in the predynastic period, he had by about 2400 B.C. become also a funerary god and the personification of dead pharaohs. With his sister-consort Isis and their son Horus, he formed the great triad of Abyddos.

The only complete account of the Osiris myth occurs in Plutarch's *Of Isis and Osiris*, although Egyptian fragments support much of his version. The son of the earth-god Geb and the sky-goddess Nut, Osiris is credited with introducing the skills of agriculture to the Egyptians. He is murdered by his brother Set, but Isis recovers the fourteen scattered parts of his dismembered body and restores him to life. Osiris, however, remains in the underworld as king, while his posthumous son Horus becomes the king of the living.

Osiris represented the resurrection into eternal life that Egyptians sought by arranging that after death their bodies would be embalmed and swathed like that of the beneficent god. Osiris is represented mummified in green stone statues, but in pictures the color of his flesh suggests that he was a black god. His body is customarily wrapped in white funeral cloths. In his hands he holds the crook and flail of kings and the scepter of the gods. The Ani Papyrus (c. 1250 B.C., British Museum) of the *Book of the Dead* shows a green Osiris enthroned, sitting in judgment over the dead, who recite before him their 42 "negative confessions."

—Norma L. Goodrich, 1997, Grolier Interactive Inc.

This cult bears striking resemblance to the legends of Nimrod, Semiramis, and Tammuz that came out of Mesopotamia at about the same historical period. The legend goes that Nimrod (Baal, lord) dies and Semiramis dismembers his body, sending the various parts throughout the world. The single exception to this scattering is his reproductive parts. Subsequently, Nimrod becomes deified and sires an equally deified son, Tammuz. We now have the ingredients for a mother-son scenario that will persist throughout the centuries. Semiramis becomes the Madonna figure, complete with halo, and holding her son of a god in her arms. Although we might

have thought that this icon originated with the virgin bearing the true Son of God two thousand years later, the Devil
evidently had his counterfeit "seed of the woman" in place as
many as twenty-three centuries earlier. Although the account
of the incident in Eden may not have been committed to a
written format at this early point in time, it was presumably
prominent in oral tradition. What later became an important
element in the biblical narrative apparently accounts for the
issuing of this "seed of the woman" legend centuries before
Jesus was born.

The westward advance of such legends might have been
limited and stifled were it not for the Phoenicians and their
merchant methods.

> The Phoenicians, called Sidonians in the Old Testament and
> Phoenicians by the Greek poet Homer, were Semites, re-
> lated to the Canaanites of ancient Palestine. Historical re-
> search indicates that they founded their first settlements
> on the Mediterranean coast about 2500 B.C. Early in their
> history, they developed under the influence of the Sumeri-
> an and Akkadian cultures of nearby Babylon. About 1800
> B.C. Egypt, which was then beginning to acquire an empire
> in the Middle East, invaded and took control of Phoenicia,
> holding it until about 1400 B.C. The raids of the Hittites
> against Egyptian territory gave the Phoenician cities an
> opportunity to revolt, and by 1100 B.C. they were indepen-
> dent of Egypt.
>
> —"Phoenicia," *Encarta Encyclopedia*, Microsoft, 1997

Note the relationship the Sidonians had with Egypt from the
earliest days of their history, about 2500 B.C. These ancient
merchants sailed their ships throughout the Mediterranean,
the Nile, and, as time passed, to ports far beyond. Among the
items they distributed were icons, figurines, trinkets, jewel-

ry, and other items for decoration of home and body. Accompanying these articles of merchandise were the legends, stories, and myths of their origination. In fact, the Phoenicians were devout pagans and they doubtless spread their religious inclinations by peddling their wares throughout the ancient world. The distribution of goods was wide. It included the entire known world and may even have extended as far as South America, the British Isles, and the Far East.

The distribution of goods was deep. Items that would be attractive and appealing to a vast market traveled by ship to and from the far reaches of the world. There was something for everyone, provided they could afford it. Exotic animals, foodstuffs, jewelry, wrought iron and other metals, the unusual, the conversation stimulus, the enviable, and the extravagant were available both in number and variety.

The distribution of goods was rich. Those items traded had much appeal so far as worldly attraction goes, including the lust of the flesh, the lust of the eyes, and the pride of life (1 John 2:16).

According to both biblical and secular history, much of the merchandise came from slave labor. The merchants purchased at a low price, but sold at enormous profit with a markup that staggers the imagination. This markup accounts for the maximized marketing of religious memorabilia and symbols throughout the Mediterranean. The observances of rituals and other forms of worship that were typical of the Canaanites produced marketable merchandise for the traders of Phoenicia to distribute first in the eastern Mediterranean, and eventually throughout western civilization.

So abominable were these observances, that the Lord eventually commanded Joshua and company to exterminate the people who practiced them. They included child sacrifice, bestiality, homosexuality, and other lewd, unnatural, and indecent acts.

Baal worship commonly took place at a temple on a hill (see 2 Kings 10:18–27). These structures were similar to the Jewish Temple, with an outer court for sacrifices and liturgy, an inside room for gathering, and a further inner room containing statuary. Sacrifices were also performed in a tower located on top of the building. As part of the ceremony, priests and participants reenacted the events narrated in the Ugaritic story. This reenactment may even have included bestiality, since Baal, the bull, is said to have mated repeatedly with a heifer before he entered the place of the dead. Following this, the worshipers participated in ritual mourning. They mourned the demise of Baal. This ritual involved loud moaning and slashing the flesh, similar to the description of Anat's mourning over Baal: "Of Baal she scraped her skin with a stone, with a flint for a razor she shaved her side-whiskers and beard; she harrowed her collarbone, she ploughed her chest like a garden, she harrowed her waist like a valley, saying: 'Baal is dead!'" (J. C. L. Gibson, *Canaanite Myths and Legends*, p. 74). This is reminiscent of the self-mutilation performed by the prophets of Baal on Mount Carmel (1 Kings 18:28). After the mourning, gladness ensued in celebration of Baal's resurrection and subsequent enthronement. Feasting, drinking, and sexual promiscuity, assisted by temple prostitutes, characterized the merrymaking.

—*Israel, My Glory*, February/March 1999, page 11

Many today claim that their willingness to bring some of the symbols and archetypes of these religious observances into their homes cannot violate God because the rituals do not accompany the practice. "We don't worship the evergreen tree, we just decorate our home with it at Christmas," is the kind of expression often heard. To illustrate how ridiculous this seems, permit me to share an ugly story with you.

At a yard sale one morning I witnessed a middle-aged woman purchasing a drinking cup with a picture of a naked woman on it. She told the clerk, "My husband likes to look at naked women on the computer so I'm taking this home to him." My mouth must have dropped completely open in shock and disbelief. This woman actually believed that since her husband did not physically engage in any tangible sex act with these "images" that it was okay to bring them into her home for him to enjoy! How utterly stupid! These images, whether on the computer or the cup, were a blatant violation of her marriage. They represented adultery and lasciviousness on his part against her. We would call that an outrage, would we not?

Then by what logic are we allowed to bring other kinds of "images" into our homes that historically and traditionally represent spiritual adultery? By what logic do we assume that images of paganism, like images of sex, are just fine so long as we do not engage in the act? How can we assume that God is not violated when we celebrate certain holidays with images that for thousands of years have offended our Father in Heaven? If Jesus Christ is the same yesterday, today, and forever, when did He change His mind about the paganistic, the pornographic, and the profane, and so transgress His essential being?

The westward movement of paganism greatly affected the Middle East. The biblical narrative chronicles the battle of the gods with reference to Israel beginning at the Tower of Babel incident. In those lands where Babylonianism reigned unchecked, however, the unbridled advance of the profane influenced everyone it touched.

One of the earliest victims of this westward movement was a city of Asia Minor called Pergamum. In Scripture, Pergamos was known as the place "where Satan's seat [throne] is" (Rev. 2:13). So how did Babylonianism migrate from Mesopotamia to Asia Minor? We already have seen that the Phoenicians contributed much to the circulation of the entire system, but other clues exist as well.

> Egypt received her science and mathematics from the Chaldeans and in turn Greece received them from Egypt. Now since the priests were in charge of teaching these sciences, and since these sciences were used as a part of religion, we already know the key as to how the Babylonish religion gained its strength in these two countries. It is also true that whenever a nation was able to overcome another nation, in due time the religion of the subduer became the religion of the subdued. It is well known that the Greeks had the very same signs of the zodiac as did the Babylonians; and it has been found in the ancient Egyptian records that the Egyptians gave the Greeks their knowledge of polytheism. Thus the mysteries of Babylon spread from nation to nation until it appeared in Rome, in China, India, and even in both North and South America we find the very same basic worship.
>
> —An unnamed Internet source

But how did Pergamos become the seat of Satan if Babylon was the seat? The answer again is in history. When Babylon fell to the Medes and Persians, the priest-king Attalus fled the city and went to Pergamos with his priests and sacred mysteries. There he set up his kingdom outside the Roman Empire and thrived under the care of the Devil.

This kingdom fell under the supervision of a succession of regents until Attalus III. In 133 b.c. he bequeathed his kingdom to the government of Rome. By 45 b.c. the priesthood fell into the hands of Emperor Julius Caesar. Thereafter, succeeding emperors inherited the office of priest and king.

Crowns in the shape of a fish head were worn by the chief priests of the Babylonian cult to honor the fish god. The crowns bore the words "Keeper of the Bridge," symbolic of the "bridge" between man and Satan. This handle was adopted by the Roman emperors, who used the Latin title *Pontifex Maximus*, which means "Major Keeper of the Bridge."

When Emperor Maximus III refused the office, the Bishop of Rome assumed the title and the garb that went with it. The pope today is often called the pontiff, which comes from *pontifex*. When the teachers of the Babylonian mystery religions later moved from Pergamum to Rome, they were influential in paganizing Christianity, and were the source of many so-called religious rites which have crept into ritualistic churches

—Ingraham, *Merchants of Tarshish*. Unpublished

Meanwhile, Pergamos (Pergamum) became the capital of Mysia with a blending of power, religion, and intellectual life. It boasted a temple dedicated to emperor worship, and Emperor Caesar Augustus is said to have often wintered here to dry out from his drunken binges in the western regions of the empire. In addition, the city was the capital for Bacchus, the god of wine. Alcohol and all its abuses dominated the culture. Pergamos was truly a throne for the Devil and his devices.

European civilization as it exists today owes much to its Babylonian origins. The various religious influences, including that of biblical Christianity, did much to shape the continent for the two millennia since the days of Julius Caesar. Most of the pagan traditions of our holiday seasons, including those of Halloween, Christmas, and Easter, bear the markings of rituals, practices, and cultural phenomena of societies running contrary to, or in direct opposition to the Bible.

This excerpt from an encyclopedia article validates the tremendous influence pagan Phoenicia, Mesopotamia, Syria, and Egypt had in shaping the cultures from which most Americans originate:

> European culture owed a great deal to its older and more sophisticated neighbors. In Greek myth Europa, the figure from whom Europe takes its name, was the daughter of Agenor, king of the Phoenician city of Tyre, and this legend expresses an important historical truth. Europe inherited or adapted many inventions or discoveries that originated among the peoples of the ancient Near East: The calendar, the art of writing, numerals, weights and measures, money as a medium of exchange, the first metallurgy, and the idea of commerce were all European imports from Mesopotamia, Syria, or Egypt. The great universal religions were Asiatic in origin, not European. The Hebraic tradition, eventually incorporated into European culture through the medium of Christianity, was one of the most profound Near Eastern influences on the West. Ancient Greece is usually considered the birthplace of democracy, but the practice of consultation in political matters appears to have been common to most nomadic tribes.
>
> —*Grolier Multimedia Encyclopedia*, "Europe I," 1998

We can be grateful that the Hebraic tradition with its Christian flavor managed to temper the pagan influences to some extent. However, we must also realize that much of what has become traditional even in the church has likewise been flavored by ungodly and perverse customs, habits, and routines. Just because "we've always done it that way," doesn't mean we were correct in doing so.

Chapter Six
Where Is Christ in Christmas?

The scene at home is that of a festive holiday. Evergreen wreaths and a fir tree decorate the house, and children nearly burst with anticipation over the gifts they will soon open. Festivity captivates nearly everybody's thoughts and plans as the holiday approaches. Even the public square reflects the greenery and garnish of the season. According to the calendar, it is the third week in December; however, two major elements seem to be missing in the scenario. First, there is no mention of Jolly Old Saint Nick with his reindeer and sleigh; and, second, there is no nativity scene, Star of Bethlehem, or "Silent Night" in evidence. What is wrong with this picture?

Nothing is wrong at all since the calendar (a little anachronism here) reads 14 B.C. The celebration is that of the winter solstice which, in the Roman scene described above, is celebrated as *Saturnalia*. Although many of the elements of the holiday fit the modern celebration of Christmas, the birth of Christ is still a decade in the future and Santa Claus will not appear on the scene for centuries.

Imagine, however, that the calendar now advances all the way to the close of the twentieth century. The birth, life, death, and resurrection of Christ are established facts. Western civilization has been both formed and vitalized by Christianity for centuries. Moreover, the impact of the Man from Galilee has been enormous both in the shaping of all of history and the shaping of millions of individual lives. Yet the most conspicuous change in this holiday setting, known for centuries as Christmas, is the interpolation of a gift-bearing and bearded figure in a red and white suit, with nine reindeer, of which one has a notable red nose. Absent from the picture is the Christ of Christmas, the creche, and the acknowledgment of the Person, Power, and Place in human history of the Son of God, Jesus of Nazareth. With the dawning of the "Age of Aquarius" has come the demise of an era dominated by the church. Ethical pluralism, moral relativism, existentialism, and chaos churn uncontrollably in the wake of the Christian age.

The preceding scenario is by no means imaginary. In recent years, we increasingly have heard of public school restrictions on holiday celebrations that mention Christ. Meanwhile, these same schools have established "replacement" holidays bereft of any reference to Jesus of Nazareth.

Among these "replacement" celebrations, some include forms of solstice worship, whose religious tone they cannot deny. However, since such celebrations avoid any reference to Christ, they comply with the "separation of church and state" requirements of modern consideration.

In one recent instance, a school in Oregon inaugurated an alternative to Christmas that should send chills up the spines of every American citizen, especially the Christian community. In the pretense of forbidding "religion" in the classroom, school officials did what is both insidious and despicable. As the school assembly program progressed, and as parents evidently looked on, a printed program became the object of everyone's attention. The cover depicted both the sun god (Lucifer, god of light) and the moon goddess (see Revelation 17, Mystery Babylon), indentifying the Babylonian origin of the rituals described within the printed program guide.

The solstice celebration that followed was nothing short of diabolical. The children engaged in chanting, dancing, and drumming, being seated in a circle according to their sign of the zodiac, and ingesting "sun and moon cake" among other occult activities. Note well that the incident occurred under the pretense of removing religion from the public school arena. Although it separated Christ from state, it clearly proved to be a state-sponsored and state-directed religious ritual. More importantly, it established a precedent that will influence public school holiday programs nationwide in the immediate future.

The irony of the matter is that the world is separating itself from the church because the church has failed to separate itself from the world. The world has found the Bible and its teachings distasteful and unacceptable. Accordingly, the world has begun to isolate and to delete what is Christian in its winter holiday celebrations. Perhaps such action will jar the church and shame it into isolating and deleting what is pagan in Christmas.

Descent Into Darkness

Biblical evidence suggests that civilization experienced great spiritual decline following the Flood, punctuated by the incident at the Tower of Babel. Paul, the apostle, writes of this spiritual declension: "Because that, when they knew God, they glorified him not as God, neither were thankful; but became vain in their imaginations, and their foolish heart was darkened" (Rom. 1:21). One consequence of man's unbelief was his intense fear of the darkness. He noticed that the sun did not shine all the time and that after the sun had set, it was dark for a long time. He had no way of knowing how long it would last and just as his fear reached its peak, the sun rose again and the cycle repeated.

Then men began to notice that although the *length* of the cycle remained constant, the amount of daylight waxed and waned as the seasons progressed. Nights began to last longer than days and men began to fear that the sun would decline completely. Then the decline stopped, the days began to grow longer, spring arrived, and man celebrated accordingly. That celebration eventually found its way backward on the calendar to December 21, the day when the sun stops its annual decline in the sky. We know that day as the winter solstice.

Cold and hunger accompanied the advent of winter. Wood and trees became sources of comfort to quell the fears of darkness. Ritual fires burned daily to coax the sun back to the summer season, and evergreen boughs and trees symbolized life and vitality in the dead of winter. These elements began to find their way into homes, caves, and public places in a heathen attempt to dispel evil spirits of darkness and death. In Babylon, the god Tammuz became associated with the seasonal cycle of death and decay followed by fertility and revitalization. Although it is difficult to document, some maintain that Tammuz was a predecessor to the Roman god Saturn. Both biblical and secular sources indicate that these practices moved westward out of Mesopotamia (Babylon) centuries before Christ. Then, with the rise of the Roman Empire came the rise of the mid-winter festival of Saturnalia, namesake of the Roman god. It incorporated all the above observances and much, much more.

Saturnalia owed its popularity to many factors. All work and business was suspended. Slaves were given temporary freedom to say and do what they liked and certain moral restrictions were eased. The streets were infected with a Mardi Gras madness, presents were exchanged, and the cult status of Saturn himself, traditionally bound at the feet by woolen bands, was untied in order to come out and join the fun (*Encyclopaedia Britannica*).

In his booklet *The Shocking Truth About Christmas*, Dr. Russell K. Tardo writes:

> . . . Saturnalia was the most vile, immoral feast that ever disgraced Rome. It was a season of license, revelry prevailed, and the entire city wantonly indulged in the filthiest sorts of immorality imaginable.

The early church found no basis for associating with such debauchery, evidently for good reason.

Nobody seems to know when Saturnalia and Canaanite religion intersected or whether, in fact, they actually did. But the emergence of what became the "Christmas tree" indicates a correlation between what the Bible depicts as worship in high places, and groves and the winter tree of Saturnalia.

Solstice and the Evergreen

Veneration of trees had begun in the garden of Eden, where one tree represented eternal life and another conveyed the knowledge of good and evil. Eve apparently became preoccupied with the fruit of the latter and, with the help of the Tempter, capitulated to what must have been an idolatrous relationship to it. Adam later acquiesced and mankind was plunged instantly into an inescapable legacy of sin and death.

Later in human history, the heathen came to believe that certain gods or spirits inhabited trees; therefore, they offered sacrifices under them: "Ye shall utterly destroy all the places, wherein the nations which ye shall possess served their gods, upon the high mountains, and upon the hills, and under every green tree" (Deut. 12:2). "For they also built them high places, and images, and groves, on every high hill, and under every green tree" (1 Kings 14:23).

Tree ceremonies were not limited to the Middle East, however. When Spanish explorers discovered the New World, they found that the Mayans of Mexico revered the cypress tree and attached offerings of teeth and locks of hair to its boughs. In China, red banners with words of praise and thanksgiving printed on them adorned certain sacred trees. In Finland, the Lapps collected samples of all the foods eaten at the solstice feast, put them into a small birch trough, and fashioned the piece into the shape of a small boat with sails, masts, and oars. They then placed the vessel into the branches of a special pine tree which had sacred symbols on all four sides. The Druids loved the oak tree as well as the fir. During the winter solstice they tied apples to the branches of these trees and thanked the god Odin for blessing them with fruitfulness. They made offerings of cakes shaped like fish, birds, and other animals. They also adorned the boughs with lighted candles in honor of the sun god.

In Roman circles, Saturnalia adopted the motif of green boughs, fir trees, fertility rites, and protection from spirits and darkness. According to one source, holly and ivy first came together in the Roman Saturnalia. They were thought to be magical in quality with the ability to repel one's enemies. Ivy was thought to bring good luck, especially to women. The combination of holly's leaves and red berries was thought to be especially effective against the "evil eye." Mistletoe became associated with fertility, connecting it with the act of kissing.

In other countries the celebration of the winter solstice assumed different characteristics. In China, little children received coins packaged in red envelopes bearing the words "New Happiness for the New Year." In Thailand, perfumed water was thrown over friends and guests as a form of greeting for the New Year. But the festival that moved westward and became amalgamated with the celebration of the birth of Christ was characteristically dominated by evergreen trees, wreaths, and boughs.

A Merger of Church and Paganism

The connection between winter solstice celebrations and the commemoration of the birth of Christ became official in the middle of the fourth century A.D. By a process known as *syncretism*, the church merged Saturnalia with the celebration of the Mass of Christ.

> During its first three hundred years, the church in Rome maintained a staunch position against all pagan beliefs and practices; however, many new and potential converts were reluctant to give up their familiar celebrations. One of the most popular holidays in the Roman year was the Saturnalia. It was a week-long festival with torchlight processions, gift giving, and merrymaking culminating in a winter solstice feast on December 25, called *Natilis Solis Invictior*, the Birthday of the Unconquerable Sun. The holiday honored the strength of the sun and the fertility it would soon bring to the earth.
>
> —Sheryl Ann Karas, *The Solstice Evergreen*, p. 88

In A.D. 375, the church announced that Christ's date of birth had been discovered to be December 25. This date was without biblical or historical grounds, however, and became official only for the sake of convenience so that the celebration of the birth of Christ could be merged with pagan festivities of the season.

The church decided on an "if you can't beat 'em, join 'em" approach to the problem. It incorporated Yuletide rituals into Christmas. The candles came to symbolize Christ, the light of the world, and the holy offerings represented the gifts of the wise men. The church attempted to defeat pagan practices by attaching them to church functions and festivals. The church intended for its influence to rub off on such paganism and so eventually Christianize the world. Instead, the world began to paganize the church.

O Tannenbaum

The *decorated* Christmas tree may have originated with Martin Luther. Legend has it that he was walking home one clear and cold evening when he noticed the stars shining brilliantly through some trees. It seemed like the stars had settled on the boughs themselves. He cut down a small tree, took it home, and placed small candles in metal holders on the branches. From this meager beginning, the Christmas tree developed, complete with ornaments, garlands, colored lights, and pastries. German Lutherans brought the tree custom to America, much to the consternation of early Puritans. Both in England and New England, the Puritans were successful in banning such remnants of the Saturnalia from public view. But eventually the Christmas tree, the Christmas stocking, and Santa Claus (borrowed from the Dutch) became thoroughly entrenched in the American holiday tradition. Now the unthinkable is happening.

Keeping Christ in Christmas

While the church is making feeble efforts to "keep Christ in Christmas," the heathen are finding Christ and Christmas (as practiced) incompatible. The school in Oregon that celebrated the winter solstice instead of Christmas, had the little children dress up in costumes as trees and animal spirits (coyotes, hawks, frogs, etc.). According to reports, kids came in with bar codes stamped on their foreheads. The bar code of some was read and accepted, but other children, who did not have the proper mark, were rejected.

Note the following connection with Scripture:

> And he causeth all, both small and great, rich and poor, free and bond, to receive a mark in their right hand, or in their foreheads: And that no man might buy or sell, save he that had the mark, or the name of the beast: or the number of his name. Here is wisdom. Let him that hath understand-

ing count the number of the beast: for it is the number of a man; and his number is six hundred threescore and six.

—Rev. 13:16–18

This connects the practice in Portland to the end-time religion of Babylon, because the false prophet is connected to the Harlot Babylon in Revelation 17.

Furthermore, Bible students for centuries have noted the apparent Christmas celebration held at the death of the two witnesses of Revelation 11: "And they that dwell upon the earth shall rejoice over them, and make merry, and shall send gifts one to another; because these two prophets tormented them that dwelt on the earth" (Rev. 11:10). This celebration may well be Saturnalia, a Roman form of Babylonianism. Considering the time in prophecy that it takes place, we can validate the belief that with the revival of the Roman Empire will come a revival of its Babylonian religious system. The seeds of that system already exist and will continue to grow.

So, how can today's Christian redeem the Christmas holiday without compromise or complicity with the bogus system that lies behind much of it? Given the foregoing information, can a legitimate celebration of Jesus' birth take place simultaneously without all the paganism that normally accompanies it? With the following suggestions to offer, we affirm with some caution that it can.

First, be aware that the traditions that accompany Christmas run deeply in western social roots. Withdrawal from the purely pagan elements ought to avoid these two pitfalls:

1) Don't make a spectacle of your attempts to accentuate the positive and eliminate the negative. Christians already run the risk of appearing antisocial just because we raise up a standard against sin. When you wear an ostentatious chip on your figurative shoulder, you invite confrontation and appear to look down your long nose at a culture that doesn't

agree with you. Somebody will invariably rise to the occasion, knock that chip away, and challenge your "holier-than-thou" attitude or appearance.

2) Make changes slowly, minimizing the pain others in your family might experience if they fail to share your conviction in the matter. The easiest items to minimize are the green decorations such as wreaths, holly, ivy, and mistletoe. Year by year, eliminate them one by one, and soon they will be history and not even missed.

The lights you display on the lawn, along the eaves of the building, in windows, and elsewhere can begin to disappear in like gradual manner. However, of all the forms of Christmas fare, these ornaments seem the least objectionable. They have little precedent in historic forms of pagan worship or activity. So if you wish to make a clean sweep, the lights can be among the later things to go, provided, of course, that they are simple lights, and not lighted pagan symbols.

The dead evergreen tree will be the most durable, immovable object of Christmas veneration. The traditionalists in your family will not release its hold without objection. The strategy that works best gradually minimizes the tree's prominence while concurrently elevating the Jesus elements of Christmas.

Begin by making the creche the central focus of the living room. Year by year, reduce the tree's visibility and centrality. Its size can dwindle to the point where it may stand best on a small table. Our family even graduated to a living and potted Norway pine tree, complete with simple decorations. After all, what does a dead fir tree symbolize? Be creative, and discover for yourself that the movement away from the profane will be a satisfying pilgrimage although it may take years to accomplish. Old habits are hard to break, especially for those not convinced they exist or need breaking.

We must turn some of our attention to that affable old elf who has established himself as the pagan god of Christmas.

Santa Claus became a commercial gimmick and a money-making device mostly during the past century. The image we have of him today began with Coca-Cola signs and advertisements early in the century. Today he is responsible for the spending of billions of dollars, the overextension of credit to the point of financial disaster, and the promotion of inexhaustible greed for an ever-increasing number of weeks per year.

Santa has transgressed the acceptable limits of fun, however, to become a pagan idol dressed in red and white. Santa has assumed divine qualities you may not have considered.

For example, who but some omnipresent being could deliver presents to every household in the world overnight? Wittingly or not, some promote his godhood by insisting he is omniscient. After all, "he sees you when you're sleeping and knows when you're awake." Right?

Furthermore, this righteous old bearded wonder demands righteousness of his followers, just like God does. "He knows if you've been bad or good, so be good for goodness' sake!"

You may laugh at this attempt to attribute idolatry to him, but consider the mind of a child who addresses old Saint Nick. The child often is filled with reverential fear—and sometimes with terror! Just visit the department store Santa and observe the smaller children. Many of them cower in his presence and shrink from him in absolute dread.

Beyond that, Santa is the provider of all good things, who demands that the child obey Mommy and Daddy (and him, vicariously through them). One false move, one bad word, one devious thought, and the Christmas tree just might be bare come Christmas morning.

Santa becomes a veritable object of worship for the child. The child writes to him, expresses his prayers to him, and addresses Santa by faith, much as we converse with the Lord. Even the adult learns to honor Santa by the sacrifices he must make to keep him alive in the mind of the child.

Then comes a day when the child realizes it was all a lie! He discovers that Santa, like the Wizard of Oz, is a phony, a part played by a man wearing a mask and pretending to be real but who is not. The jolly one in whom the child believed was part of a ruse, perpetrated and perpetuated by parents who also lied about the whole thing.

These same parents may also have told the child about Jesus Christ. We come to Him by faith, and we worship and obey Him, also. But, if both Santa and the Wizard were lies, where does this leave the True God and the Lord Jesus in the mind of the child? Did Mom and Dad lie about Him too? Why should the child believe in the invisible God and the Lord Jesus when at least two other objects of their faith proved to be insidious phonies?

In no small way, the veneration of Santa is tantamount to idol worship. He is a false god. We train our children in idol worship when we fail to tell them the truth about Old Saint Nick—a serious departure from the faith indeed!

In our family, we told the truth about Santa from the earliest beginnings. Far from being devastated and devoid of joy, our daughter joined right in with other children, pretending Santa was real, but knowing he is not. She got all the enjoyment of the season, but without any disillusionment. As other children grew to realize the truth, she revealed she knew it all along and it was okay. She accepted Jesus at age five and never faced any conflict about His reality and importance.

Must we avoid the celebration of Christmas? Can't we salvage *something* of the season? Of course, but learn to discriminate between sacred and secular, pure and profane.

First of all, give gifts. God did. First, He gave His Son to expiate sin; then He gave eternal life to those who believe on that Son. Exchanging gifts symbolizes a godly kind of love. Giving and love are synonymous terms in biblical Christianity. The best definition of love is "giving to the highest good of another." That's what typifies God's love for us; that should typify our expression of love for those around us.

Christmas comes at a time of year when ministries and missionary agencies often ask for end-of-year gifts of support. Use your own judgment about the propriety of giving in the light of tax breaks and financial advantage. But, since we claim to be celebrating Jesus' birthday, how appropriate it is to give Him a gift by supporting His work!

Do Christmas cards seem important to you? Must you ignore family and friends who send them to you? Of course not! This is an excellent opportunity to share a brief word of testimony, send a family photo, and remind your Christmas card list that Jesus is the reason for the season. Nevertheless, be discreet about the content of your cards and limit them to biblical themes where possible.

Jesus and His generation attended festivals and gatherings. Where appropriate, we all can do the same. Family and friends seem especially important during the holiday season. Whether you attend such gatherings or host them, be sure to make meaningful social contacts during Christmas. Your friends and family may comment on the absence of certain seasonal items if you host the occasion. Explain that you've begun to minimize some aspects of Christmas in order to maximize others that are more important to you.

You need not follow the adage, "when in Rome, do as the Romans do" so far as your social contacts outside the home. Be discreet, be kind, be yourself. Don't sacrifice your principles for the sake of going along with the crowd. On the other hand, where gray areas exist, try not to be so black and white.

Gifts, Christmas carols, nativity scenes, conservative parties and gatherings—all can be a part of your celebration when handled with discretion. If you are mature enough to be appropriately concerned about these matters, you likely are mature enough to make appropriate decisions about them.

Chapter Seven

The Ongoing Battle

Much can be written about the battle waged between the prophets of Israel and their confrontations with Baal, Babylon, and the entire realm of paganism. Among the earliest such dramas is the one that takes place at Mount Carmel. Here, one of the nonwriting prophets encounters the prophets of Baal whose champion is Queen Jezebel, wife of Ahaz. During this scenario, the four hundred fifty false prophets were unable to rouse Baal and summon him to consume a sacrifice. An additional four hundred false prophets of Asherah (the grove) likewise were helpless to rain fire down upon the sacrifice, demonstrating the impotence of their gods. Elijah wet the wood on his altar to the true God by pouring four jars of water over it three times. In response to Elijah's prayer, Yahweh rained fire from heaven and consumed the wet wood. Elijah ordered the false prophets killed for their deception (1 Kings 18:19–40).

Even earlier in Israel's history, the Lord had confronted an occult practice that originated in Babylon now called necromancy, or consulting with the dead (1 Sam. 28). King Saul, needing a word of counsel from Samuel, supposedly recalled him from Sheol for consultation. He subsequently learned from the apparition that such practice was not an acceptable option. Scripture had consistently forbidden such an encounter. The departed Samuel reinforced this as he evidently appeared to King Saul through the witch of Endor (Exod. 22:18; Lev. 20:27; Deut. 18:10–12). Nothing in divine revelation sanctioned such a practice nor indicated such a communication was possible. King Saul, therefore, had learned of it by means of the religious practices of his day in the land of Israel. Indeed, the presence of a witch whether in Endor or elsewhere was a clear violation of God's covenant with His ancient people: "Thou shalt not suffer a witch to live" (Exod. 22:18).

The practices of witchcraft, sexual acts with animals (Exod. 22:19), and sacrificing to other gods (Exod. 22:20) were probably all connected with Canaanite fertility worship which is a derivative of Babylonian religion. Moreover, if this seance was real, then it is the only such case in Scripture and an instance where a prophet after death was able to confront a Babylonian practice.

Elsewhere, the biblical prophets confronted paganism with a unified voice. A consistent theme of their treatment is to demonstrate the utter futility of fashioning an idol from one part of a tree then warming yourself with the fire from another part of the same tree. Isaiah tells us the land of the covenant was overrun with idolatry at the time of his writing, about 700 B.C.: "Their land also is full of idols; they worship the work of their own hands, that which their own fingers have made" (Isa. 2:8).

He then describes the foolishness and futility of worshiping a god fashioned by one's own hand or the hand of some craftsman: "They that make a graven image are all of them vanity; and their delectable things shall not profit; and they are their own witnesses; they see not, nor know; that they may be ashamed" (Isa. 44:9).

Their folly is self-evident and obvious from the above verse.

Who hath formed a god, or molten a graven image that is profitable for nothing? Behold, all his fellows shall be ashamed: and the workmen, they are of men: let them all be gathered together, let them stand up; yet they shall fear, and they shall be ashamed together.

—Isa. 44:10–11

The craftsman labors and expends his energy; yet the dumb idol cannot sustain him, feed him, or quench his physical thirst. Isaiah must have had a smirk on his face despite the tragic nature of his discourse.

The smith with the tongs both worketh in the coals, and fashioneth it with hammers, and worketh it with the strength of his arms: yea, he is hungry, and his strength faileth: he drinketh no water, and is faint.

—Isa. 44:12

Not all idols were made of metal or stone. Among the finest were those fashioned from wood by the carpenter: He carefully plans his work, designs the image with his compass, and fashions a figure for the god that is fully human. Little wonder that the unbeliever accuses us of making God in our own image rather than the other way around. Note well that the tree from which he fashions this image is a product of the Lord, His sun, and His rain.

The carpenter stretcheth out his rule; he marketh it out with a line; he fitteth it with planes, and he marketh it out with the compass, and maketh it after the figure of a man, according to the beauty of a man; that it may remain in the house. He heweth him down cedars, and taketh the cypress and the oak, which he strengtheneth for himself among the trees of the forest: he planteth an ash, and the rain doth nourish it.

—Isa. 44:13–14

The practice of cutting a tree from the forest and bringing all or part of it into one's house for reasons *other* than burning for warmth or cooking predates the birth of Christ by nearly twenty-three hundred years. Although there is no direct correspondence between that practice and what millions of us do during the Christmas season, an indirect similarity certainly exists.

> Then shall it be for a man to burn: for he will take thereof, and warm himself; yea, he kindleth it, and baketh bread; yea, he maketh a god, and worshippeth it; he maketh it a graven image, and falleth down thereto. He burneth part thereof in the fire; with part thereof he eateth flesh; he roasteth roast, and is satisfied: yea, he warmeth himself, and saith, Aha, I am warm, I have seen the fire: And the residue thereof he maketh a god, even his graven image: he falleth down unto it, and worshippeth it, and prayeth unto it, and saith, Deliver me; for thou art my god.
>
> —Isa. 44:15–17

In case the reader is about to dismiss all of this and ascribe it to Old Testament times, permit us to quote from the apostle Paul in his Mars Hill speech:

> Forasmuch then as we are the offspring of God, we ought not to think that the Godhead is like unto gold, or silver, or stone, graven by art and man's device. And the times of this ignorance God winked at; but now commandeth all men every where to repent.
>
> —Acts 17:29–30

Truly, such idolatry is ignorance; nevertheless, it is no longer an ignorance that the Lord overlooks or ignores. We must keep ourselves from any form of such activity and practice because it merits the judgment of God.

Because he hath appointed a day, in the which he will judge the world in righteousness by that man whom he hath ordained; whereof he hath given assurance unto all men, in that he hath raised him from the dead.

—Acts 17:31

As for the idolaters of Isaiah's day:

They have not known nor understood: for he hath shut their eyes, that they cannot see; and their hearts, that they cannot understand. And none considereth in his heart, neither is there knowledge nor understanding to say, I have burned part of it in the fire; yea, also I have baked bread upon the coals thereof; I have roasted flesh, and eaten it: and shall I make the residue thereof an abomination? shall I fall down to the stock of a tree? He feedeth on ashes: a deceived heart hath turned him aside, that he cannot deliver his soul, nor say, Is there not a lie in my right hand?

—Isa. 44:18—20

According to verse twenty, the idolater feeds off futility; he is the victim of deception; he is lost and too blind to perceive the falsehood he practices. We are not intolerant of such people; we only wish to help them see themselves the way others do.

The prophet Jeremiah makes a similar observation to that of Isaiah: "For the customs of the people are vain: for one cutteth a tree out of the forest, the work of the hands of the workman, with the ax" (Jer. 10:3). The futility of worshiping idols appears here in graphic detail. While decorated with silver and gold (v. 4), an idol is still the product of man. It cannot move or speak and can do neither good nor evil.

The reference is *not* to a Christmas tree; however the similarity cannot be ignored. We decorate the evergreen tree with garlands of various types, with decorous bulbs, and trinkets made to look like gold and silver. Then we fasten it to the floor in such a way that it cannot fall over.

> They deck it with silver and with gold; they fasten it with nails and with hammers, that it move not. They are upright as the palm tree, but speak not: they must needs be borne, because they cannot go. Be not afraid of them; for they cannot do evil, neither also is it in them to do good.
>
> —Jer. 10:4–5

Many of us are anxious to protest that at Christmas time we do not worship the tree, nor do we commit any pagan practice. Our attention is invariably focused on the child of Bethlehem, not on the accoutrements of the season.

Meanwhile, we are quick to call him Scrooge or Grinch who marks for us the paganish origins of what we practice at the Christmas season. We rationalize our practice by insisting that what once may have been a pagan tradition now has the sanction of God because we use it to celebrate the birth of His Son. We deny any guilt about celebrating the Son with the holiday trappings of a religious system far removed from anything biblical. Satisfied that we have answered the critic with an element of sanctimony, we turn a blind eye to the questionable aspects of our holiday celebrations.

For example, we seem blind to the fact that the evergreen tree has been a symbol of Tammuz for nearly four thousand years. Although Tammuz is the god of vegetation, he experiences annual death in autumn and resurrection in the spring. His continuing presence and a reminder of him during his winter absence is the evergreen tree, his abiding symbol until the greenery of spring emerges. Whether in the form of a tree or that of a wreath made from its boughs, the evergreen represents paganism in a big way.

We seem to forget that mistletoe and holly are fertility

symbols that for centuries accompanied orgiastic celebrations including those of the winter solstice and Saturnalia. In fact, our Christmas celebration is fashioned according to the festival of Saturnalia. Many of our traditions, including office parties and other holiday excesses, often employ similar activities and practices to those of antiquity.

We have noted elsewhere that the burning of the yule log connects to the festival of Samhain (Halloween). Yet many of us merrily and ignorantly sing our "fa-la-la-la-la's" about it during the holiday season.

Despite all of this and more, we continue to hear from even the most pious among us that what we now do to celebrate Christmas and other holidays is just fine with God. After all, we are doing it for Christian, not pagan reasons.

When Jereboam raised the two golden calves in the northern kingdom, he did it in order to provide a place of worship for his people. Do we ever read that God approved such action? Jereboam rationalized his use of these golden idols much the way we rationalize today. He did the wrong thing for a right reason—but it remained a wrong thing regardless of the reason. "And the times of this ignorance God winked at; but now commandeth all men every where to repent (Acts 17:30).

Ezekiel confronted paganism rather extensively both in his daily personal ministry and in the biblical book bearing his name. Like other prophets both contemporary with and preceding him, Ezekiel denounces idolatrous practices and pronounces judgment on those who practice idolatry in Israel. The Jews of antiquity made a flimsy pretense of worshiping the Lord, but openly embraced paganism. Isaiah earlier had said:

Wherefore the Lord said, Forasmuch as this people draw near me with their mouth, and with their lips do honour me, but have removed their heart far from me, and their fear toward me is taught by the precept of men.

—Isa. 29:13

Idolatry must have been widespread and common because the punishment seemed to have been pervasive:

Thus saith the Lord God; Smite with thine hand, and stamp with thy foot, and say, Alas for all the evil abominations of the house of Israel! for they shall fall by the sword, by the famine, and by the pestilence. He that is far off shall die of the pestilence; and he that is near shall fall by the sword; and he that remaineth and is besieged shall die by the famine: thus will I accomplish my fury upon them.

—Ezek. 6:11–12

The places of worship seem familiar. Many of them appear in the verses cited below:

Then shall ye know that I am the Lord, when their slain men shall be among their idols round about their altars, upon every high hill, in all the tops of the mountains, and under every green tree, and under every thick oak, the place where they did offer sweet savour to all their idols.

—Ezek. 6:13

Israel, like the heathen around them, worshiped the sun, moon, and stars, and even employed the zodiac in their pagan practices. Evidently, the Asherah (the grove) stood in the temple area, as if to provoke the Lord to jealousy.

And he put forth the form of an hand, and took me by a lock of mine head; and the spirit lifted me up between the earth and the heaven, and brought me in the visions of God to Jerusalem, to the door of the inner gate, that looketh toward the north; where was the seat of the image of jealousy, which provoketh to jealousy.

—Ezek. 8:3

Ezekiel next saw the abominations of Egyptian and Canaanite animal worship, called here the "idols of the house of Israel," portrayed on a wall.

So I went in and saw; and behold every form of creeping things, and abominable beasts, and all the idols of the house of Israel, pourtrayed upon the wall round about. And there stood before them seventy men of the ancients of the house of Israel, and in the midst of them stood Jaazaniah the son of Shaphan, with every man his censer in his hand; and a thick cloud of incense went up.

— Ezek. 8:10–11

Jaazaniah was a member of a prominent family, "the son of Shaphan," a leader in the administration of Josiah (cf. 2 Kings 22:3–5). As the leaders committed abominations before the Lord, they led their people down a path of sin and destruction. They violated the covenant God made with Moses at Mount Sinai and soon found themselves evicted from the land given to Abraham, Isaac, and Jacob.

The most startling confrontation between the godly and the pagan among the prophetic books is that of the three Hebrew children and the idol that Nebuchadnezzar established in the plain of Dura in the land of Babylon. "Nebuchadnezzar the king made an image of gold, whose height was threescore cubits, and the breadth thereof six cubits: he set it up in the plain of Dura, in the province of Babylon" (Dan. 3:1).

This image was ninety feet by nine feet—a ten to one ratio. This may have been a human image, representing the king, because the word used for "image" in the Aramaic is a general word. But for that reason we might also conclude the image was an obelisk, because the proportions fit the obelisk better than any human figure. Only if the ninety feet include some significant pedestal for the base of the image could the king's image be thought to correspond. Of course, the king took his cue from Daniel's interpretation in which the king was the head of gold. The king wished to extend his term in power by extending the gold all the way through the image.

The False Prophet will establish an image for people to worship as the Tribulation enters its mid-point. Enforced state religion will require those who fail to fall in obeisance to the image of the Beast to meet a fate similar to that proposed for those who failed here in chapter three of Daniel.

Emperor worship has come and gone throughout the times of the Gentiles. The latest such worship included Japanese Shinto worship and Russian worship of Lenin.

Idolatry and all its trappings should be met with resistance, not compliance, by those who call upon the name of the Lord. When they were confronted by the raging king for resisting his demands for worship, the three Hebrew children replied that the Lord would deliver them, but even if it meant death, they would not acquiesce to his enforced idolatry. In their case, the Lord made their deliverance most obvious. The Lord Himself defied the king and the king took notice.

> The attempt of this great king of Babylon to unify the religions of his empire by self-deification will be repeated by the beast, the last head of the Gentile world-dominion (Rev. 13:11–15). See "Beast, the" (Dan. 7:8; Rev. 19:20). It has repeatedly characterized Gentile authority in the earth, e.g. Dan. 6:7; Acts 12:22, and the later Roman emperors.
>
> —Scofield note on Daniel 3:1

And the people gave a shout, saying, It is the voice of a god, and not of a man. And immediately the angel of the Lord smote him, because he gave not God the glory: and he was eaten of worms, and gave up the ghost.

—Acts 12:22–23

The minor prophets with one voice dismiss the practices of the heathen as exercises in futility. The minor prophets denounce idolatrous folly with great clarity and emphasis (Hos. 13:2; Hab. 2:18; Zeph. 1:3; and Zech. 10:2).

They likewise declare divine retribution upon those that practice false forms of worship and who violate the First Table of the Law given on Mount Sinai (Hos. 8:4, 10:1; Mic. 1:7, 5:13; Nah. 1:14; Zeph. 1:3; Zech. 13:2). Our immutable Lord has proclaimed these pagan practices, accoutrements of worship, and acts of sacrilege to be sinful and unacceptable. Whether we duplicate them exactly, or even in some oblique way incorporate these pagan elements into our holiday seasons, our immutable Lord would seem to be offended and our walk with Him diminished.

Incidentally, the judgments so eloquently pronounced by the prophets of God finally came. To the Northern Kingdom they came at the hands of the Assyrians in 722 B.C.; to the Southern Kingdom they came at the hands of the Babylonians by 586 B.C. While other reasons for judgment may have contributed to the downfall of the divided monarchy, there can be no doubt that pagan Babylonianism was a major factor as cited by the prophets.

Following the captivity and upon the return of Israel to the land circa 536 B.C., idolatry ceased to be a major concern in Israel. It seems that the people had their fill of paganism as they had lived in all its excesses for the seventy years of captivity. Evidently, they had seen from the retributive hand of God upon them that serving Him must be done in singleness of heart and not in the duplicity they had hypocritically practiced in previous times.

Other problems would emerge in the spiritual life of the Hebrew nation, but idolatry and pagan practices would only prevail outside the boundaries of Israel. The Gentile world would have to await the emergence of Christianity before the Lord would emphatically confront paganism among the nations. Alas, the "mother" church of the Dark Ages would eventually fail miserably in its responsibility to separate the sacred from the secular; the proper from the profane.

It falls, therefore, to the church of Jesus Christ today to make those distinctions and draw lines of demarcation between what is acceptable and what is not in the realm of worship and the ambassadorship afforded us by our soon-coming Lord. We must not fail as others have done in the past.